SEN

The Shaping of the Welfare State

R.C. Birch

LONGMAN

Longman
1724-1974

LONGMAN GROUP LIMITED
London

*Associated companies, branches and
representatives throughout the world*

First Published 1974

ISBN 0 582 35200 2

Printed in Great Britain by Whitstable Litho, Whitstable, Kent

Contents

Introduction to the Series

The seminar method of teaching is being used increasingly. It is a way of learning in smaller groups through discussion, designed both to get away from and to supplement the basic lecture techniques. To be successful, the members of a seminar must be informed — or else, in the unkind phrase of a cynic — it can be a 'pooling of ignorance'. The chapter in the textbook of English or European history by its nature cannot provide material in this depth, but at the same time the full academic work may be too long and perhaps too advanced.

For this reason we have invited practising teachers to contribute short studies on specialised aspects of British and European history with these special needs in mind. For this series the authors have been asked to provide, in addition to their basic analysis, a full selection of documentary material of all kinds and an up-to-date and comprehensive bibliography. Both these sections are referred to in the text, but it is hoped that they will prove to be valuable teaching and learning aids in themselves.

Note on the System of References:

A bold number in round brackets **(5)** in the text refers the reader to the corresponding entry in the Bibliography section at the end of the book.

A bold number in square brackets, preceded by 'doc' **[docs 6, 8]** refers the reader to the corresponding items in the section of Documents, which follows the main text.

PATRICK RICHARDSON
General Editor

Acknowledgements

We are grateful to the following for permission to reproduce copyright material:

The Executors of Lord Beveridge for an extract from *Causes and Cure of Unemployment* by Sir William Beveridge; the Estate of the late Lord Beveridge and Hodder & Stoughton Ltd for an extract from *Beveridge and His Plan 1954* by J. Beveridge; Cambridge University Press for four extracts from *Men without Work* by the Pilgrim Trust; Frank Cass & Co. Ltd for extracts from *English Poor Law History* by B. & S. Webb, reprinted by permission of the publishers Frank Cass and Co. Ltd London 1963; Cassell and Company Ltd and Houghton Mifflin Company for an extract from *The Second World War* Vol. IV by Winston S. Churchill; the Controller of Her Majesty's Stationery Office for an extract from *Problems of Social Policy* by R.M. Titmuss and an extract from *Report of the Committee on Local Authority and Allied Personal Services* Cmnd 3703 (1968); The London School of Economics and Political Science for extracts from *Our Partnership* by Beatrice Webb; Macmillan, London and Basingstoke and St. Martin's Press Inc., for an extract from *Life of Joseph Chamberlain VI* by Julian Amery; The Society of Authors, on behalf of the Bernard Shaw Estate for an extract from *Major Barbara* by Bernard Shaw; The Times Newspapers Limited for an extract from 'the first leading article' from *The Times* of 1st July 1940: reproduced from *The Times* by permission, and the Author for an extract from *Documentary History of England 1965* by E.N. Williams.

PART ONE

Background

1 Introduction

The term 'welfare state' has become a commonly accepted description of modern British society. It is not an attractive term, and it is not now a fully adequate one; but it will not be easy to replace since it has come to tell us a good deal about that society. It expresses, first, a concern for the individual, with formal schemes to compensate for loss of earnings through sickness, unemployment and old age, and a health service to provide medical care for all regardless of means. It implies, second, a degree of collectivism, with the State framing national policies in the interest of the community as a whole, maintaining a high level of employment, providing decent housing, a favourable environment, and a system of education in which no talent is wasted.

There has, however, been little welfare state philosophy, like those associated with socialist or fascist structures; not even a body of ideas like those surrounding the nineteenth century capitalist state in its heyday. In fact, if, as is commonly accepted, the phrase was first used by Archbishop Temple, it was meant by him to point a dramatic contrast between the rigidly organised and unfree fascist state and the compassionate yet free society that Temple and so many others looked forward to in the dark years of the Second World War; 'in place of the conception of the Power-State we are led to that of the Welfare-State' (4). It has not been consciously created, and it does not conform to a system of ideas, and the nearest we have ever come to a welfare state philosophy was in that same feeling for a new world which held the people of Britain together in those years. The parts of its structure are everywhere evident today, but they have no common architectural pattern. It has grown gradually, and both the whole and its components have suffered change. There have been long periods of barely perceptible growth, and in the natural calamities of war and depression there have been feverish attempts to extend its shelter; yet there has never been any fundamental agreement about its meaning or purpose.

Socialists, on the whole, share a common outlook. The builders of the welfare state have been men and women of utterly different beliefs, backgrounds and persuasions. They have compromised with each other, and their purposes have been limited by the forces which have opposed

3

them; what they have created is itself a compromise as their efforts have been diverted into channels which they did not seek. Yet, in sum, what they have done is to steer society into ways which it would never have followed had it been left to itself and the free play of economic forces. This complex growth has therefore led historians to disagree about the relative importance of the forces which have gone to make it, about how far we should look back for its origins, and about the precise way in which this shaping of modern society has taken place; and these differences have in turn contributed to modern political arguments about the role it should now play and the future path it should take. Both past and present are full of paradox. 'Why', asks David Roberts, in his study of the Victorian origins of the British welfare state, 'did England create an administrative state which she did not want?' **(31)**. Is it further, today, the true purpose of the welfare state 'to teach people how to do without it'? **(56)**.

Yet whatever their disagreements about the origins of the British welfare state, few historians would dispute its uniqueness, for it is one that derives from its close connections with other powerful forces in British history. The recovery, in the nineteenth century, of some of the paternalism of the Tudor state, was compounded of the humanitarian and Benthamite response to industrial conditions which Britain was the first nation to encounter. It produced that peculiar form of collectivism which created statutory policies in the fields of industry, public health and education and reconstituted a harsh Poor Law to deal with personal poverty; and these were extended and adapted in the twentieth century, under the lash of depression and total war, and turned to the more sympathetic relief of destitution. This fusion of traditions ensured that there would never be a wholly 'state' welfare; and the liberal tradition of the nation was strong enough to modify the growth of social democracy in such a way that the provision of welfare involved only a qualified collectivism and a limited redistribution of wealth, that it ensured subsistence without creating full economic equality, and left the opportunity for a man to do as much for himself as possible.

It also brought forward a new understanding of liberty that is perhaps peculiarly Anglo-Saxon. The Majority Report of the Poor Law Commission of 1905-09 declared that liberty, in the light of the desperate poverty of those years, had become 'a mockery and a falsehood' [**doc. 14**]. Political leaders, alarmed by the obvious cracks in the British social structure that were appearing in the first years of this century, were seeking to combine the individualistic virtues of the nineteenth century with the shadowy yet, to many, sinister socialist ideas of the twentieth. Churchill maintained that freedom had become incomplete 'without a measure of social and economic independence'. In 1912, Woodrow Wilson suggested that it was 'something more than being left alone. The program of a government of freedom must in these days be positive, not negative merely.' Perhaps its finest expression was to come with Franklin Roosevelt in 1934: 'Government has the definite duty to use all its powers and resources to meet new social problems with new social controls — to insure to the average person the right to his own economic and political life, liberty, and the pursuit of happiness' (23). In Britain, a tradition of self-help and political freedom, and the incredible adaptability of the governing class throughout history, ensured that social progress would be gradualist; a reasonable balance had therefore to be achieved between the fruits of private enterprise and the provision of public welfare.

This process of compromise has brought an essentially practical, even cynical, view of the development of the welfare state. At the lowest level, it has been seen merely as an insurance for the continuation of the profit motive; a little higher, as a prudent modification of the natural interplay of economic forces that would preserve political and social stability; and, better still, as an attempt to put right the ills of an industrial society which had developed with little concern for the welfare of the ordinary man (59). In these terms, the degree of 'social and economic independence' of which Churchill spoke, would be the minimum compatible with the preservation of an old form of society. Yet some, fewer in number, have seen it as the road to a new form of society which would make the optimum provision for all its members, and not just a patched-up version of an old one. For them, the vital period in the story of the welfare state is held by the years between 1940 and 1948, when the full impact of war transformed British society [docs 24, 26, 27].

War made individuals important, especially young ones. It made them members of a vital community in the effort they were inspired to make together to defeat the common external enemy in a cause most felt to be right. War exposes the shoddiness not only of the administration of a nation, but of the ideals which sustain it; it gives the high emotion which binds men in a common purpose and it provides the idealism through which change may be effected (6). The postwar Labour Governments gathered this harvest; they all but destroyed the old, locally administered Poor Law and created social services that were original in their integration and universality. Yet even before their defeat in 1951 came the inevitable reaction from the tight government that had been necessary to war and readjustment. Community spirit ebbed, and there was a renewed demand for freedom and initiative. Full employment and a more secure personal wealth do not promote the growth of social ideals. The visionaries of the war years may well have believed that they were creating a new order on egalitarian foundations; but nothing done by the Attlee administrations came really near to changing the basis of society. With the growing comfort and the lessening pressures of the postwar years came the view that the social policies of the Labour Governments marked the end of a chapter, the successful conclusion of a long struggle, even that the welfare state belonged to the past from which it had emerged.

Against this background the future path of the social services could not fail once again to be surrounded by compromise. Behind the arguments of the 1950s about public and private responsibility, about cost, freedom of choice and universality, were deepseated political attitudes which depended largely on value judgments which were not susceptible to proof. Yet the debate of those years was still conducted very much in terms of the past, and behind it was a profound ignorance of the real nature of the society which had emerged and of the way in which it would grow; and with little awareness, therefore, of the way in which social policies would have to develop. There was far from precise knowledge about who really paid for the social services, about who gained most from an increasing state expenditure, about those whose needs were still not met, and why this was so. It would be possible, in the apparent affluence which coloured the thinking of the time, to allow men to build for themselves on the basic minimum the state provided; but there was little understanding of the fact that this could only be done within the framework of an effective universal system, or that an entirely new method of cash provision would have to be evolved so that it could be achieved without many of their fellows, even in a prosperous society with a high priority for welfare, falling below the standard of living enjoyed by the majority, or that this same affluence and welfare would produce social problems and social casualties entirely of its own, which would require as much careful investigation as had ever been devoted to simple poverty in the first half of the century.

The old disputes seem almost part of history itself, with a period flavour of their own; and they are giving way to an understanding of the fact that even in a wealthy state it is still far from inappropriate to talk in terms of shared burdens, although the task now is not that of contriving how scarcity can be made bearable but how affluence may be more commonly enjoyed. Beyond this, there is the widening glimpse of the field of welfare which lies beyond the mere satisfaction of material wants, in which it is hoped that serving and giving will become as important as the act of receiving. In this, it may well be argued that against the changing political background of our times the most appropriate field for social action of this sort is no longer the impersonal state, acting in a national framework for a national purpose, but in the immediate community where it could be conducted with greater knowledge, skill and sympathy through both statutory and voluntary agencies [doc. 28]. This is the trend of welfare in our age, and it involves to a large degree a striking reversal of the historical process. The creation of the Welfare State was achieved at the expense of a locally and often unsatisfactorily administered Poor Law. The building of an even more compassionate society may well involve the reintegration of its better elements.

2 First Steps

THE POOR LAW

Simple poverty, however, was for long at the heart of the development
of the welfare state. The Tudors were bringing forward the new nation
state, and they saw its fabric endangered by the collapse of religious
charity and the onset of economic depression. The great Elizabethan
consolidating statute of 1601 drew the guidelines of poor relief until
Speenhamland, seeking to provide work for the unemployed, practical
training for pauper children, and help for the aged, the sick and the
infirm. The undeserving poor were set aside and were given harsh treatment. The problem had been recognised – for there were clearly those
who were unable to look after themselves; and the pattern had been
set – for the parish was designated as the centre for relief. Equally
important, however, were rudimentary measures to stabilise food
supplies and prices, the encouragement given to charity, and the
exhortations to wealthy subjects to make endowments to schools,
hospitals and almshouses. Thus began an attack on poverty that was to
last until the nineteenth century – by the Poor Law, locally administered,
and by private charity, both assisted by a general supervision from the
centre that would not outlast the Civil War, but which would reappear
faintly in the nineteenth century when local administration began to
break under stress and charity had been proved insufficient, and much
more strongly in the twentieth, when the more general aspects of Tudor
policy would return [doc. 1].

The range of Poor Law activities widened down to 1834. Parish
doctors were called in to cases of sickness; houses were sometimes found
for the poor, and rents made up or wholly paid; the poor were buried
at the public expense, and in these ways the rudiments of welfare were
added to charity. But after 1660 poor relief became more than ever a
local matter, for the overthrow of the Stuarts weakened the central
power of the state, as it was designed to do, and there was less national
concern for social problems; the Laws of Settlement of 1662 confirmed
the local character of relief, and the quiet society of the eighteenth
century may well attest to its effectiveness. Further, if the victory of
Parliament, sealed in 1689, brought a new concept of public admini-

stration, so did the Reformation and the subsequent rise of Puritanism bring a harsher element into social thinking. The rise to power of the local gentry had limited the national concern with poverty; the promotion of the new virtues of diligence and thrift checked the stream of charity, and linked destitution with idleness and irresponsibility. The attitude was reflected in legislation. The pauper's badge appeared in 1697, and when in 1723 two or more parishes were permitted to unite in order to build workhouses, their declared purpose was simply that of putting the poor to work, and the measure led to a stringent workhouse test. Yet it is worth noting that here for the first time the limitations of the parish itself had become apparent.

Into the second half of the eighteenth century, however, breaks the humane feeling that was to alter social attitudes so radically. A static and complacent age gave way to a dynamic and troubled one. Artists and writers like Hogarth and Smollett began to look beneath the serene surface; the charitable, like Coram and Hanway, became more aware, and the insistence of Wesley and Wilberforce on an active Christianity gave the age a new purpose. There was a political response. Gilbert's Act of 1782 tempered some of the harshness of the workhouse test, and it was with Pitt's blessing in 1795 that the Laws of Settlement were eased. Yet a vital motive here was the need for a more mobile labour force; necessity accompanied humanitarianism, and to it also we must add the fear and alarm of the propertied classes – a not uncharacteristic combination in the promotion of welfare – for Britain had entered the period of uncertainty and unrest which began at the end of the American War in 1783 and would last through into the nineteenth century. The demands of the French Wars increased the strain of early industrialism and of agricultural decline, producing a common people angered by the growth of machinery and enclosure, and at the same time growing politically more conscious. The turn of the century thus saw that strange mixture of repression and relief; the suspension of *habeas corpus* in 1794 was followed by the widespread adoption of the system of alleviation first introduced by the magistrates of Speenhamland in 1795 [doc. 2].

Speenhamland, by relating poor relief to the price of bread and the size of a man's family, firmly and generously established the system of outdoor relief which Gilbert's Act had envisaged. Its provisions for the making up of low wages did something to achieve the policy of the minimum wage which Samuel Whitbread, the radical, had vainly urged on Parliament in 1796 and 1800. It was widely adopted, once Parliamentary authority had been given, and its full use in the rural areas owed much to the awareness of the landowner of the appalling consequences of enclosure — some social historians have even hinted at a species of ransom; and its extension into the manufacturing areas underlines a general concern for good order. It was indeed costly, but it may have been a burden that the ratepayer was prepared to shoulder in order to avert revolution.

By 1830, however, its very scope brought wide public discussion. Criticism came from many quarters, and after 1834, when the first 'alarm' of the nineteenth century had passed, it brought a new harshness into British social policy. Ricardo and the *laissez-faire* economists preached the necessity of a low-wage economy, which Speenhamland clearly controverted; Malthus asserted that to relieve poverty was merely to increase it, and create a dependent pauper population; the Benthamites insisted that the parish was too small a unit to deal with poverty, and that there should be a national policy based on the deterrent principle of 'less eligibility'. The ratepayer, only too conscious of his burden, the industrialist, seeking to pull labour into the towns, even the landowner, uncomfortably aware that the agrarian riots of 1830 had occurred in precisely those areas where Speenhamland was strongest, all were caught up in the demand for a new method and a new harshness. A political response came with the Whigs in 1830, and with it the growing awareness above all else that the social and economic conditions by then apparent would demand more than local solutions.

EARLY VICTORIAN SOCIETY

It was the first appearance of modern industrial society that made the welfare of the people — the 'Condition of England' question — such a vital issue. The urban factory system was establishing itself, producing forces so disturbing that in facing their challenge a thoroughly individualistic early Victorian society would slowly advance towards that collectivism which has become the accepted pattern of our own age. For while poverty, disease, crime and ignorance had always existed, never before had they been so concentrated and never before had they affected so many people. Between 1801 and 1851 the population of England and Wales doubled: that of Manchester and Salford alone went from 90,000 to over 400,000. The local agencies entrusted with the health and safety of society found the task beyond them; and systems like Speenhamland, although by no means without effect upon the plight of the poor, operated wastefully and with many local variations. A new need had arisen, and there were new ideas at hand to meet it. Victorian social reform began after the passing of the Reform Act of 1832, and the years down to 1854 saw the partial introduction of some of the features of the modern welfare state. In 1833, as David Roberts has pointed out, few governments did less than the British in the promotion of social welfare; by 1854, few had achieved so much **(31)**. The period is therefore a vital one.

The Industrial Revolution did more than set the problem of concentrated poverty. It produced the wealth and technology without which social change cannot come; it brought forward an industrial working class, growing more conscious of the part they were playing in producing that wealth and of the new opportunities opening up before them; it produced a middle class which, for whatever reason, would attack social problems with purpose; and it also produced, in reaction, a determination on the part of the landowning class to strike back at the middle class which threatened to supplant it, to insist at least upon a minimum of factory improvement. It gave an edge to the pressure of the Utilitarians and it deepened the passions of the humanitarians like Sadler, Oastler and Ashley, and these two movements together provided the cutting edge of the forces that would transform the Victorian state.

In so far as the Utilitarians named pleasure, or wellbeing, as the chief end of man, and believed that if men were set free to seek their own betterment the resultant of all these improving forces would be the achievement of the 'greatest good of the greatest number', they were clearly underwriting the prevailing *laissex-faire* ideas of the age; just as in economic terms Peel and Cobden believed that in the end economic freedom would lead to prosperity and that all would share in it. Yet in the sense also that much dead wood would have to be hacked down before men could enjoy that freedom, and that barriers had to be removed from the achievement of the good, Benthamism also implied some degree at least of state intervention. This, and the Utilitarian passion for efficiency, is a vital step in the development of the collective state. Chadwick, Bentham's most famous disciple, with his genius for investigation and administration, went far along this road, and constantly reminded the middle classes of the vast drain on the national wealth imposed by disease, crime and poverty. From the abolition of negative restraint to the creation of positive programmes of public health, order and education — where the Benthamites led the campaign to make it free, compulsory and secular — was a considerable step which helped to create the atmosphere in which the seeds of the welfare state could grow **(24)**.

The Poor Law Amendment Act of 1834 is the most significant of the Benthamite statutes **(34)**. For while it set out to diminish poverty with its famous principle of 'less eligibility', and thus conformed to one of the basic assumptions of a robust early Victorian society, there can be no doubt also that it created an administrative method of enormous

11

importance for the future. The Poor Law Commissioners of 1834 constituted the first effective national agency set up to deal with a social problem; it worked through parochially elected Guardians; and this combination of central and local bodies was to provide the essential pattern of future social reform. It also created an inspectorate whose role was to be a vital one; and it inaugurated an administrative sequence — that of inquiry, followed by report, followed by legislation, followed by inspection — that was to be imitated in the attempts to deal with the social problems of the years ahead. While there were many impulses towards reform in the nineteenth century, most were cast in the Benthamite mould.

Yet neither simple humanity nor the passion for efficiency should be exaggerated, for while their exponents were an active minority, they were a minority none the less. Their creeds gained acceptance because of a general and much less doctrinaire mood which knew no party or sectional divisions and which has proved to be of enormous importance in the making of the British welfare state. It is marked by an impatience with intolerable conditions, and it is made up of a conscience aroused by the suffering of the poor, an instinct for order and safety affronted by the potential danger of the Chartist mobs, and a sense of self-preservation alarmed by the dreadful epidemics which swept through the new industrial areas [doc. 3]. Reform born of feelings like this will be limited and defensive — 'safe and necessary' — and the instinct on which it was based was not new. It had inspired the Tudors and the magistrates who met in the Pelican Inn in Berkshire in 1795, and it was part of a long tradition of sound and rational English government. What was new was that in an utterly different sort of society, fresh social and administrative channels would have to be provided for its transmission.

The process went on piecemeal. The zeal of the reformers collided with a traditional fear of centralisation, a liberal suspicion of state intervention, and a morass of self-interest. No new collectivism was created, but old and new agencies were used together to limit the worst abuses of the age. The economic theories of the early Victorians were modified by their consciences and their concern for public safety. There was limited progress, if all too often there was deadlock, as in the field of public education, where the fear of central control, and inter-denominational conflict were for so long decisive. New central bodies like the Poor Law Commission and the General Board of Health super-vised the work of local officials who exercised all too much autonomy, and they often conflicted with the older organs of local government; these were administratively weak, for otherwise there would have been no need to replace them, but they were politically strong and stubborn and rooted in the entrenched tradition of local independence. Such were to be the battles in the evolution of the welfare state.

The main battlefield in the 1840s, yielding an excellent example of defensive reform, was in the area of public health. Inquiries and Government reports, like those of the Select Committee on the Health of Towns in 1840, the Sanitary Condition of the Labouring Classes in 1842 [doc. 3], and the two reports of the Commission of Inquiry into the State of Large Towns and Populous Districts of 1844-45, set the familiar Benthamite pattern; but of far greater moment was the fear stimulated by the cholera epidemics of 1831-33 and 1847 and the typhus outbreaks of 1837 and 1839. Local impulses, aided by separate Acts of Parliament, had begun the long process of ensuring the provision of sewerage and a fast flow of clean water, but these older agencies were powerless before the appalling problems of the new age. The Public Health Act of 1848 did indeed create the General Board of Health; but it was permissive in that local Boards of Health need not be set up unless the death rate in that area was more than 26 per thousand or unless more than 10 per cent of the ratepayers wanted one. In spite of the logic of the full Benthamite case, that better sanitary conditions would bring greater order and safety and increased prosperity, the local Boards worked in vain against the power of vested interests, the incompetence of local officials, and the failure of the Act to insist on the appointment of Medical Officers of Health. As a fully independent and useful body the General Board of Health lasted only six years; it was emasculated in 1854 by the political pressures of its opponents, with *The Times* leader of 1 August 1854 maintaining that it was better 'to run the risk of cholera and the rest than be bullied into health'. Such sentiments show how little the age understood the responsibilities that society would eventually have to assume.

Yet, with little intention to transform society, much was achieved by a small group of zealots – civil servants, doctors, inspectors, and public-spirited individuals of all kinds, who helped to provide in piecemeal fashion the glimpses of a new administrative state. They inspired an impressive list of Royal Commissions and Select Committees; they produced a powerful and dedicated inspectorate whose reports added to the overwhelming case for reform and whose example helped to push it along [doc. 4]. The existence of powerful hostile interests and the ill-defined relationship between local and national government brought weakening compromise, hampering the making and execution of policy by bodies with little real power and starved of funds and staff. By 1854 the condition of the towns was appalling still; schools and workhouses were in a deplorable condition, and far too many would have to take their chance with 'cholera and the rest'. Yet in spite of all this, 'the early Victorians were the first in world history to experience the full consequences of the Industrial Revolution, and the administrative measures they took to meet them constituted the first beginnings of the welfare state which is today a distinguishing feature of the British Government' **(31).** The mid-1850s marked the heyday of the careless Palmerstonian liberalism; reform became unfashionable, for the immediate dangers of the 1840s were over and the worst evils of the age had been checked. But when the age of high prosperity had passed, and Victorian self-confidence had ebbed, there was in existence a simple, if illogical and cumbersome, machinery for improvement, so that when social conditions grew worse it would not be impossible to provide further instalments of reform.

LATE VICTORIAN COLLECTIVISM
For the moment, however, a confused tangle of old and new agencies for reform collided with a powerful individualist ethic, and much more would have to be achieved in order to modify it significantly. The stigma of poverty remained, for pauperism was a social status, involving loss of freedom, self-respect and franchise, with access merely to whatever help an overburdened Poor Law could provide. If the first years of the century had seen the task of the reformers as that of separating the genuinely poor from the lazy, it would be left to succeeding years to make the treatment of poverty more effective and more humane. The idea would die hard that the true aim of social reform was that of making the poor more independent, less ignorant, and, in sum, more 'moral'.

Dicey, in *Law and Public Opinion in England,* published in 1905, isolated the years between 1865 and 1900 and called them the 'Period of Collectivism', and defined collectivism as action by the state, even at some loss of individual freedom, to improve conditions for the people as a whole. More recent writers, like David Roberts, would not make so sharp a distinction, insisting that the legislation of the early Victorian years with its new administrative devices had begun a powerful movement for reform whose own momentum would carry it into the second half of the nineteenth century. This qualification must be accepted, yet without forgetting that the second half of the century did make a distinctive contribution of its own to the advance of collectivism, and on an appreciably wider front than before. The legislation of Gladstone and Disraeli between 1867 and 1885 marks a watershed, for while it reflects the assumptions of the immediate past, it also provides clear glimpses of the future. The work of Gladstone's first ministry in general, with its attack on privilege and its attempts to open up Victorian society, fulfilled many of the aims of mid-century *laissez-faire* radicalism; yet on the other hand, the Education Act of 1870, with the Government's insistence on properly constituted School Boards, once more underlined the limits of sporadic local and voluntary action, and with its concern for the welfare of the child and the overriding social and economic needs of the State, it illustrates a marked advance in the form and spirit of the collectivist principle [doc. 5]. Disraeli's social reform of 1874-80 achieved very little in the face of a traditional suspicion of centralisation and the powerful claims for local independence and low taxation within the Conservative Party; yet the public health legislation of those years marks a real change from negative, piecemeal interference towards a more constructive programme.

Perhaps more significantly, and beneath the surface of government, the spirit of enterprise was waning and new forms of collectivism were appearing in other spheres. The pathway to the all-embracing state was made easier by the growth of collective action and demands in the component parts of society. There were now, for example, bigger concentrations of power on both sides of industry. The trade union movement, again very largely as the result of the work of Gladstone and Disraeli, was moving from its mid-century individualistic and self-help associations, numbers were increasing rapidly, and the larger unions of unskilled men would demand more from the state than legal protection; they were becoming wedded to the principle of collective bargaining and looked for greater instalments of more positive social reform. On the other side, limited liability had fostered the growth of much larger industrial and commercial concentrations, which would soon be looking for greater intervention by the state in economic affairs, some, in the end, seeking full protection. This new collectivism in the two major forces of modern society would contribute towards forcing the state into a similar pattern (28). An overt clash between capital and labour might have been disastrous to the progress of the gradualist social reform which has marked the growth of the welfare state, had not other powerful and modifying forces been at work.

The growth of democracy, made safe by careful extensions of the franchise and the protection of the vote through the ballot, ensured that the state would go on encouraging the unions in the ways of legality they had chosen in the 1850s, and it also ensured that Parliament would be in touch with the conscience of the age and with the demands of the new radicalism. The development of education, which went essentially with the progress of democracy, produced a reasonably responsible electorate. A benevolent state was forced to watch over these developments; isolated legal attacks upon the status of the trade unions in the depressed and dangerous period of the '90s, when capital and labour were at each other's throats, and which culminated in the famous Taff Vale case, were set aside by statute in 1906; and similar attempts to restrain the School Boards from using their funds in the development of secondary education were confounded by the Balfour Act of 1902. The process was empirical, but as a democratic parliament came to grips with the problems of the early twentieth century, so the forces making for a sensible collectivism became stronger. For all these reasons, it was not likely to take the form of socialism – with which the welfare state has nothing in common – or of a highly Conservative protectionism, in which social reform was merely dispensed, in Bismarckian fashion, by an entrenched privileged class. The British welfare state did, of course, depend on a response from those in government; yet it also grew from sensible and moderate democratic pressures from below. It was an unique fusion of traditions.

Men had not forgotten Joseph Chamberlain's 'Unauthorized Programme' of 1885, which, with the Irish Question, stretched nineteenth-century Liberalism to its breaking-point [doc. 6]. When he spoke of its aim of securing 'to every man his natural rights, his right to existence, and to a fair enjoyment of it', he was already on the threshold of the twentieth century. Chamberlain had referred to his programme as 'Socialism' (28). He did not, of course, mean this in the accepted sense of the word, but his use of the term is significant. Governments, it was implied, must act with the welfare of the people in mind; at the very least, the term had to be annexed in order to destroy the challenge of its real sponsors. The mood of the earlier years is clearly changing; the force of religious intervention in social matters was so much more clearly on the side of the people [doc. 8]; and political philosophy, expressed through T.H. Green and John Stuart Mill moved decidedly in the direction of collectivism. Green, in reaction against *laissez-faire,* reasserted the principle of the community as a corporate body of which individuals and institutions were a part, and maintained that the aim of collective wellbeing was more important than the pursuit of private interests; Mill, the son of James Mill, a devout Utilitarian, extended much farther the Benthamite ideas of how the organised community could promote the interests of its members while still preserving much of the liberty of the individual.

The matter became far from academic in the closing years of the nineteenth century when the appearance of mass unemployment brought all to the test. In 1886 the poor demonstrated in Hyde Park and Trafalgar Square; the socialist societies grew in numbers and membership; and the new unions, celebrating their success in the Dock Strike of 1889, became more militant. Although there was a general swing to the right in politics in the 1890s, as property sought to protect itself, conscience was again aroused, and it would, in the early years of the new century, led by the revived Liberal radicalism, make constructive efforts to bend the state still further to meet the challenge [doc. 12]. At the same time, the path taken by the British working-class movement itself also contributed significantly to the progress of limited social reform. It turned its back on Marxism, despite the pushing of the Social Democratic Federation, and thus it rejected a political philosophy which denied the necessity for the powerful state − which therefore could not be an effective instrument for welfare. True socialism insisted on a radical reorganisation of existing society; and in a redistribution of wealth which by itself would bring benefits to all; and its adherents ceaselessly maintained that welfare benefits tossed down by governments of states in which the old social and economic framework remained intact were no more than sops to preserve that framework and prevent the spread of revolutionary ideas among the people. The British trade union movement had come of age in the period of high prosperity; broadly, it accepted the capitalist organisation of industry, and sought merely to gain the best possible advantages for its members from it. It had seen its members enfranchised and its institutions protected by a state which seemed benevolent in its intentions. British socialism was in fact collectivism, protected by the state in much the same way as the Friendly Societies; and while, as the unions expanded, a genuinely Marxist fringe would go on resisting this natural trend, the mass of the Labour movement, with the unions at its base, worked for gradual amelioration, not revolution. Fabianism, with its Benthamite passion for investigation and solution, with its acceptance of the structure of society, and with its gradualist and permeating approach, provides its most accurate illustration; and Fabianism and Benthamism together have made the most significant contributions to the development of the welfare state (42). Where trade unionism has in some degree cut across, the wider purpose of state welfare has been in the expression of the belief that collective bargaining can do more to raise the standards of the working people than political reform; on these grounds, the syndicalists challenged the parliamentary stand of the Labour leadership before 1914, and it was in this respect that Ernest Bevin expressed his reservations about the Beveridge Report in 1942 (39). The British working class has not at all times been united in its attitude to state welfare, and there is evidence today that the high wage agreements which have been reached after the pressure of the more powerful unions have hindered the raising of the general standards of the mass of the ordinary people − although here, again, it is assumed that the state will look after the interests of those left behind.

These are long term trends; political responses before 1906 were limited and still mainly local. The central bodies did what they could. The Local Government Board had been set up in 1871 to coordinate the welfare activities of local agencies, and these, after the radical overhaul of local government between 1882 and 1894, were able to widen their scope. Chadwick had always envisaged such a partnership, and the movement towards 'municipal socialism' at the end of the nineteenth century rested on the use made by zealots like Chamberlain in Birmingham of the permissive central legislation that had been inspired by men like Richard Cross. The twentieth century would till more deeply, but it would be in ground prepared by Bentham, Mill and Green, by Chadwick and the Webbs, by Dickens, Kingsley, Mrs Gaskell and Shaw [doc. 9]. More example, and certainly more revelation would be required before the new age would come fully to accept the logic of their thought and work, and look for national, as opposed to local, solutions.

CHARLES BOOTH

It is in this sense, that as the century turns, Charles Booth, the Liverpool shipowner and manufacturer, emerges as one of the most significant figures of the age. He pushed it very far towards a solution of the late Victorian dilemma: between the belief that the widespread relief of poverty undermined personal responsibility and fostered immorality, and the growing certainty that the very existence of that poverty threatened the political and economic foundations of the state. His influence was the greater in that his work was not partisan. It did not prejudge, as the Benthamites did; he wrote with none of the fury of Hyndman, who, Booth said, filled his report on poverty in 1885 with incendiary statements; he did not promise the new heaven of Marxism; he had little time for the collectivism of Beatrice Webb or the improving aspirations of Octavia Hill and the Charity Organisation Society (29), [doc. 7]. He simply showed, without the romantic imagination of Mayhew, that over 30 per cent of the people of London were living below a very low minimum of subsistence. This was done by means of patient inquiry stretching from 1886 to 1903. He did not preach. The clarity of his arguments and the force of his conclusions carried a powerful message of their own.

He spans the centuries, because while he remained an individualist, he insisted that 'the individualistic community on which we build our faith will find itself obliged for its own sake to take charge of the lives of those who, from whatever cause, are incapable of independent existence up to the required standard, and will be fully able to do so **(5)**. In his contribution to the long-drawn-out inquiries into the plight of the aged, beginning with the Royal Commission of 1893, he estimated, on the basis of his survey of the Stepney Unions, that between 40 and 45 per cent of old people were living in desperate poverty. He himself advocated a pension of five shillings a week at sixty-five; and in the end, when no progress was made after a later inquiry in 1898, he and Chamberlain signed a minority report in favour of action. As early as 1891 he had maintained that such help would 'give a surer footing to those who, now trying to stand, too often fall and sink altogether' and which 'will stimulate rather than weaken the play of individuality on which progress and prosperity depend'.

But Booth's importance to the twentieth century is wider than his contribution to a revived Liberalism. He is the pioneer of dispassionate social investigation, although his importance here became obscured when sociology took the path of social philosophy, from which it has long emerged. He set an example to a younger generation which was in itself more socially aware, as Beveridge testified **(39)**. He broke through the barrier of resignation, and by relating poverty to its environment, he undermined the view that it was due to personal or moral failing. Of even more significance, perhaps, was his contribution to the understanding of the causes of poverty. Although he contributed little to the Royal Commission on the Poor Law, and was offended by the passion with which, it seemed to him, Beatrice Webb and her supporters were distorting the end of rational inquiry, he offered an interpretation of poverty that was to have far reaching effects on its treatment in the twentieth century; the belief that the level of existence of the poor was most threatened by the competition of the very poor. It reinforced his pleas for 'limited socialism', a phrase that was not always understood, but which carried the hope that the individualistic virtues of the nineteenth century could be blended with the collective hopes of the twentieth **(doc. 10)**. This was a position which would also colour the Liberal attitude to reform in 1906, an axiom which Lloyd George might well have taken for his starting-point.

PART TWO

Development of the Modern Welfare State

3 The Formative Years

THE TURN OF THE CENTURY

Revelations of poverty multiplied as the new century opened. Rowntree, in the more favoured York, discovered a level of dire poverty comparable with that suggested by Booth, and Leo Chiozza Money, in his influential *Riches and Poverty*, in 1905, gave wide publicity to both. If the strikes of the 1890s had alarmed the rich, they had also aroused their consciences, for they were inevitably accompanied by further disclosures of the appalling day-to-day life of the poor. The 'sweated industries', those countless undertakings too small to be within the reach of factory law and with little or no union organisation, particularly captured the imagination of the public after the findings of the House of Lords Committee of 1888, the researches of Beatrice Webb **(46)**, and the exhibition organised by the Liberal *Daily News* in 1906.

The conclusion of the Boer War in 1902 brought a new thread into the developing pattern of social policy. A good cross-section of the nation was medically examined for the first time; records of a high rate of rejection caused widespread alarm, and while they were modified somewhat by the official Inquiry into Physical Deterioration of 1904, the evidence still suggested a senseless, heartless waste of human resources. Here, perhaps for the first time, is the suggestion that social reform could husband the strength of the nation in a competitive modern world, a growing theme among Conservative reformers **(36)**. Thus, as the individualism of nineteenth-century Liberalism was challenged by collectivism on the one hand, so was its internationalism threatened on the other by the rise of the pre-1914 nation-state with its concern for national welfare. It may not be too extreme to discern a link between this and national survival, an idea which has had common currency in our own century and is not confined to Britain alone; certainly, there was a growing feeling that imperial greatness and individual degradation went ill together **(25)**. The major Conservative statesman of the day, Joseph Chamberlain, indeed saw the task of good government as that of developing national and imperial resources of all kinds, and in his programme of Tariff Reform – which did so much to destroy the Conservative administration in 1905, open the way for a revived Liberalism, and yet remain as a serious alternative to it — the promotion of national prosperity and personal welfare was a major theme [doc. 11]. Not only the nation's conscience, but the nation's pride was being stirred.

The work of the Conservative governments down to 1905 reflected a little of these ideas. They had, again at Chamberlain's prompting, been responsible for the pioneer legislation on Workmen's Compensation in 1897; it did not for ten years include seamen, domestic servants or farm workers, and in securing compensation men were often involved in costly legislation, but it marked a beginning. The Unemployed Workmen Act of 1905 did little more than try to coordinate relief, establish destitution committees in large towns, and give local authorities permission to levy a small rate to provide work; it did not extend into the areas of destitution uncovered by Booth, and it made no attempt to remedy the weaknesses of the Poor Law. The Conservatives were still tied to permissive legislation, still hampered by local independence and a resistance to higher taxation, but their leader, Arthur Balfour, could none-the-less discern a case for social reform and firmly distinguish it from socialism itself, 'its most direct opposite and its most effective antidote'. Yet it was the Conservative neglect of the social question and their alleged attack upon the standards of the poor, both in the matter of their daily living and in the status of their trade unions, which gave the real edge to the election campaign of 1905. A reborn Liberalism shed many of its old individualist associations. 'There is much that the State can do which is not only consistent with liberty but essential to it.'

This might have been said by almost any prominent Liberal leader of the time. It is, in fact, an extract from the Majority Report of the Poor Law Commission of 1909.

THE ROYAL COMMISSION ON THE POOR LAWS AND THE RELIEF OF DISTRESS 1905-9

The Commission set up in 1905 by the outgoing Conservative administration grew only partly out of the growing concern with poverty. It came more from the feeling in administrative circles than in the changing conditions of the twentieth century the old Poor Law, particularly as it applied to the able-bodied, was under intense strain, and that, in so far as the primary aim of the disbursement of public assistance was to decrease the number of those requiring it, it was not achieving its purpose. Its members were chosen with some imagination and formed a good cross-section of those concerned with the social problems of the age; it contained the permanent heads of the Local Government Boards

23

of England, Scotland and Ireland, whose task it was to supervise poor relief, together with representatives of the trade unions, religious bodies, charitable organisations – and the formidable Mrs Beatrice Webb of the Fabian Society. Its terms of reference did not contain the possibility of the destruction and supersession of the Poor Law and of the ideas which sustained it, but rather its modification, and the removal from its jurisdiction of certain categories of unfortunates, a process already haltingly begun. This was not enough for a minority of its members, including Beatrice Webb and the Labour movement's George Lansbury and Francis Chandler, and this difference in outlook was reflected in the eventual production of two reports instead of one [docs 14, 15]. The split was a radical one, and Mrs Webb, the moving spirit among the smaller group, was convinced from the first meeting that whatever changes in structure might ensue, the principles of 1834 were going to be reaffirmed, and the Commission 'spoon-fed by evidence carefully selected' (46). In reaction, she took the proceedings a long way towards an inquiry into the causes of destitution [doc. 13].

The Commission was of little immediate significance. Both reports are of vast importance, however, in that they crystallise past, present and future attitudes to the whole question of poverty; and while we are assured that Lloyd George did not read it until 1911, both the Conservative legislation of 1929 and that of the Attlee Governments after the Second World War owe much to the combined statement of the Commission. Both sides agreed that the Poor Law would not serve in its existing form; the majority because it had been wasteful, impersonal and unwieldy, the minority because it had sustained a shaming pauperism for too long. Both suggested the transfer of some of its functions to local authorities; although the minority advised the setting up of specialist committees.

While, however, the majority wished to modify the principles of 1834 and to alter the structure they supported, the Minority Report rejected them altogether. The Majority Report clung to a modified form of 'less eligibility', and sought to give most weight to more stringently controlled voluntary agencies, under a Committee of Voluntary Aid, joined with reformed public services transferred to counties and county boroughs; the minority, doubtless under the influence of the Webbs' Fabian centralisation, wanted the state to assume the major role, working through local government bodies, and using the voluntary societies as much or as little as they wished. The majority, under the influence of the Charity Organisation Society ('one of the most typical of mid-Victorian offspring' to Beatrice Webb), wanted to preserve an element of moral discrimination in the treatment of poverty;

they favoured the encouragement of insurance, with the deserving poor, that relic from the past, looked after by the voluntary agencies, and the less deserving dealt with by reorganised Poor Law Authorities, to be renamed Public Assistance Committees, in a somewhat harsher way; throughout the proceedings, the impression is strong that the attitude and findings of the majority were coloured by a concern with the peripheral causes of poverty, such as drunkenness, immorality, and indiscriminate charity [doc. 7]. Behind the Minority Report, by contrast, was the Fabian assumption that the causes of poverty were social, and that if it was a moral problem, it was not connected with the failings of the individual but with the shortcomings of society itself – the 'crime' of poverty attacked by Shaw in *Major Barbara* [doc. 9] – and that by sound and enlightened social policy destitution could not only be relieved, but abolished. They did not favour insurance, since the doling out of allowances with no appropriate treatment attached, was a most unscientific form of state aid [doc. 17].

They resisted strongly the setting up of a Destitution Authority, or whatever it was to be called, of the old Poor Law type. They wanted the Poor Law to be destroyed, and its work transferred to local specialist committees concerned with education, health, and so on. Central direction of these, however, was to be vital; there should thus also be a Ministry of Labour and a network of labour exchanges to prevent and lessen the incidence of unemployment; industrial training and public works in time of depression; and the general aim of securing that national minimum of subsistence below which no one should be allowed to fall [doc. 16]. The state should therefore develop specialised and technical services of every sort, and this is the direction in which the Liberal statesmen of the period were already moving with Care Committees for children, the School Meals service and similar agencies, and it is by and large in this specialist form that the welfare state has developed in our own times.

The sole purpose of the Minority Report [wrote Beatrice Webb], "so we told listeners and readers, was to secure a national minimum of civilised life [note the word minimum] open to all alike, of both sexes and all classes, by which we meant sufficient nourishment and training when young, a living wage when able-bodied, treatment when sick, and a modest but secure livelihood when disabled or aged" **(46).**

In the story of the welfare state, the place of the Webbs is secure, for words like these foreshadow the work of the postwar Labour Government of 1945-51. Yet, in fairness, the signatories of the Majority Report

were not blind to the appalling social conditions of the age; they
favoured the diversification of the monolithic Poor Law administration,
and suggested a strikingly novel casebook — or 'case-paper', as they
termed it — method of social investigation. They may also have sensed
something which the minority, in their reforming zeal, lost sight of:
that in the old Poor Law there was a function of relief which the modern
welfare state is only now regaining. However badly, and with whatever
motives, the old system approached the problem of poverty on a family,
and not an individual basis, interpreting care in a very wide sense indeed;
and when under the growing influence of the ideas expressed in the
Minority Report, the Poor Law grew weaker and its old and often
rudimentary local agencies were replaced by more impersonal and often
national ones, a valuable potential was lost. The voluntary local agencies
which the majority sought to build up might have provided it. It is now
widely believed that a good deal of social work is more effective when
applied on a family basis, and that even the individual is best dealt with
in the family setting. It is this which the modern welfare services, since
the Seebohm Report of 1968, have tried to recreate [**doc. 28**] **(76)**.

LIBERAL ACHIEVEMENTS, 1906-14

The Minority Report of the Poor Law Commission set out an ideal.
Political realities were different. The Liberal leaders were conscious
enough of the distress of the time and a number of them were personally
close to the Webbs; and they were also aware, by 1908, that their first
years in power had yielded little. The Conservatives, angered by the
magnitude of their defeat in 1905, and convinced that the Liberals were
dangerously close to the new force of Labour, had from the start used
their huge majority in the House of Lords to blunt the reforming edge
of the new Government. Piecemeal reform had improved the status of
merchant seamen and children, in the case of the latter moving towards
that subtraction from the Poor Law that was among the Commission's
original aims, and the trade union disabilities imposed by the Taff Vale
decision had been removed; but if these measures had done little to
improve the material condition of the people, they had done much to
harden the attitude of the opposition.

An even sharper decline in living standards had become apparent in
the first six months of 1908, when unemployment, rising to over 7 per
cent, was nearly double the average for the last ten years. Radical
suggestions also increased. Extremists in the Labour movement demanded
industrial action, and the number of strikes multiplied. The election of
1905 had strengthened the proportion of Tariff Reformers in the

Conservative Party, and they insisted that if the country were to return to Protection unemployment would fall as foreign competition declined [doc. 11]. Liberal measures, by contrast, seemed undramatic, and by-elections indicated a turning of the political tide. Political and economic necessity thus counted as much as the pressure of social reformers, and Government changes in 1908 brought into prominence the two men who would do most, in these years, to improve the lot of the 'left-out millions'. The phrase is that of Winston Churchill, who became President of the Board of Trade when Lloyd George succeeded Asquith at the Exchequer. The latter, now Prime Minister, gave steady support to his younger colleagues, but it was they who were to become the outstanding political figures of the century – so deeply concerned in all its issues that they could not but play a major role in this one. Of course, they freely used the ideas of others, but they made them real when they had reached what Stanley Baldwin would later call 'the threshold of acceptance'. Beatrice Webb equivocally called them 'mendicants for practicable proposals', but they saw clearly what was possible, and they used their whole energy and skill to become the political pioneers of the Welfare State.

Lloyd George was the first Cabinet minister to have been born in poverty, and he attacked it with a passionate hatred. At the same time, he was ever acutely aware of the challenge of Labour and of the need to meet it [doc. 12]. Churchill, too, had a flair for catching the mood of the times, and a supreme gift for expressing it.

> I do not want to impair the vigour of competition, but we can do much to mitigate the consequences of failure. We want to draw a line below which we will not allow persons to live and labour yet above which they may compete with all the strength of their manhood. We do not want to pull down the structure of science and civilisation – but to spread a net over the abyss. And I am sure that if the vision of a fair Utopia which cheers and lights the imagination of the roving multitudes should ever break into reality, it will be by developments through, modifications in, and by improvements out of, the existing competitive organisation of society. **(41)**.

There is something here of Beatrice Webb's national minimum of subsistence, but added to it is the politician's awareness of the difficulty of rapid and radical change – the contrast between the desirable and the possible that has become a commonplace in the twentieth century. Yet Churchill was sincere, deeply attached to the memory of his father, whose radicalism the Conservatives had rejected twenty years before.

27

He had joined the Liberals because of his belief in Free Trade, and he understood the power of Protectionist ideas as instinctively as Lloyd George, from his humble background, saw the moral and emotional challenge of socialism. The Liberals had to find their own answer to the problems of distress, to find another and more acceptable basis for the modern state which was emerging. The battle for political and economic freedom had been won by men like Gladstone in the nineteenth century; that for social freedom, for a decent standard of life for the people at large, was about to be joined.

Churchill was not long at the Board of Trade, but his record here is a proud one. His first concern was for the depressed and unorganised workers in the so-called 'sweated industries'. No powerful unions defended them, and factory law had passed them by; and as Charles Booth had discerned, they were 'a body of reckless, starving competitors for work', pushing down wages and standards for the working people as a whole. His Trade Boards Act of 1909 went a long way towards establishing minimum wage rates in these trades. But politicians did not build the welfare state alone, and Churchill brought into prominence two outstanding public servants, typical of so many who were to play an honourable part in the making of the social services. Sir Hubert Llewellyn Smith, Permanent Secretary to the Board of Trade, who knew the problem of poverty from his work at Toynbee Hall, began to construct the pilot scheme of unemployment insurance which Churchill developed after 1908 **(41)**. On the advice of the Webbs, who had high hopes of the young Winston, Churchill called in William Beveridge, an Oxford don of twenty-nine, who had already won a reputation for his academic work on poverty and distress. He too, had a slight link with Booth, for he later wrote that it was under his influence that Edward Caird, Master of Balliol, had entreated Beveridge and others of his generation to discover why unprecedented prosperity should still produce such poverty **(39)**. Like the Webbs, Beveridge was a convinced believer in the idea of labour exchanges, and supplied Churchill with the framework of his plans.

The new mood of the Liberals had been marked by the introduction of Old Age Pensions in 1908, when Asquith's last budget set aside £1,200,000 for the purpose. The scheme began in 1909, with five shillings a week paid to old people over seventy; they were to draw the full benefit as long as their means did not exceed £21 per annum, and proportionately less up to a ceiling of £31.10s. The scheme was non-contributory, for Asquith had no wish to make the old wait for a qualifying period and did not wish to trample on the interests of private companies. The problem had been recognised for years; now it had been dealt with, and the community had come to the rescue of destitute old age. Churchill stuck to the theme of poverty in the months that followed, and his speeches are full of references to the plight of the casual and unskilled labourer, as well as to that of the skilled man laid off in times of slump. Beveridge had already insisted in *Unemployment, A Problem of Industry*, 1909, that unemployment, with proper national care, was not a necessary accompaniment of industrial development, and he had told the Poor Law Commission that the social problem of the age was not only unemployment but underemployment, and the Commission had in fact marked it out as 'the original fountain of so many of the greatest evils in our social life', a view of the majority with which the minority concurred. Both represented a chronic disease. Insurance against unemployment, maintained Churchill, would relieve a little of the burden of destitution. The setting up of labour exchanges would make some beginning at least to a national distribution of the work available, and guide young people especially into worthwhile jobs.

The first labour exchanges were set up in 1910, but Churchill advised Asquith that plans for unemployment insurance should wait until Lloyd George had made progress with his scheme for health insurance. It appeared, with few modifications, in Part II of the National Health Insurance Act of 1911, which called for a weekly levy of twopence from all workers in the scheme, with one penny each added by the employer and the Treasury. It was to apply to something over two million men in the seven trades most affected by depression, chiefly in building, shipbuilding and engineering, and they were to be paid, when out of work, an average of a little over six shillings a week up to a limit of fifteen weeks. The scheme was to support itself; there was no question of help from general taxation; the amount of benefit was not enough for a bare living, and there was little hope of help, beside the voluntary agencies and the Poor Law, beyond the given period. It was merely a lifebelt, and it would not hold up the unemployed in the deep and dangerous seas of the postwar depression, but it was a marked advance on the shadowy beginnings of 1905.

Lloyd George's difficulties had been caused by his deep involvement in a political and constitutional struggle that was to play a vital part in the story of the welfare state. In 1909 he had introduced the most radical budget ever to come before Parliament. The need for naval building, and the Liberals' determination to press ahead with social reform, led to proposals for heavier and more varied taxation than ever before. The Conservatives were faced with a plan for the redistribution of income designed to support a programme of advanced radicalism, and the Chancellor introduced it with the attitude of one who blamed the established order and the capitalist economy for having tolerated inhumane conditions for too long. To the Liberals, it was the key to further progress; to the Conservatives, it was the thin end of the wedge of Socialism, the first step towards not the 'welfare state' but the 'servile state'. The issues surrounding social progress in the twentieth century were stated clearly for the first time. The House of Lords behaved recklessly, as perhaps Lloyd George intended, for they threw out the Budget and precipitated a serious constitutional crisis. The Liberal Government prepared a Parliament Bill to reduce the powers of the Upper House, and the Lords accepted the Budget the better to oppose it. The loss of two general elections in 1910, a bitter campaign in which Lloyd George and Churchill led the attack on privilege, particularly that associated with land, and Asquith's use of the royal prerogative in threatening the creation of new peers, brought Conservative opposition to an end.

The Budget and the Parliament Act, a financial measure and a constitutional reform, thus have immense social significance. With the first, Lloyd George had forced the acceptance of the principle that the wealth of the nation must be shared out more fairly by taxation. The second had broken through the hard outer crust of the opposition to future social progress. Both were as essential to the growth of the welfare state as the National Health Insurance Act which followed in 1911.

The principle of personal insurance against sickness had been accepted for a long time, and some six million people were insured either by their trade unions or by friendly societies. But the latter alone had a record of a quarter of a million lapsed policies each year, and many of them were far from sound. Lloyd George simply proposed that the community should make up for these deficiencies in a system of national insurance. Like so many at this time, he was concerned at the prevalence of tuberculosis. It had killed his father, and it was killing some 75,000 Britons each year. It was the disease of squalor; yet it called for expert medical care. It thus, in some degree, helped to link the public health reforms of the nineteenth century to the concern for personal health which has marked the twentieth. Yet much political skill would be needed to pass any measure of health insurance. If the Conservatives feared Socialism, the doctors were worried lest a public scheme threaten their professional independence and reduce their incomes – although history has often been less than fair to them, for they also were concerned about the health of the community, and about the millions spent by the people on often worthless patent remedies, and many of them already played a major part in the voluntary 'dispensing societies' already in existence. But most hostility came from the friendly societies and insurance companies, who saw the danger that much of their business would be taken away.

The Act insured against loss of health and made provision for the treatment of sickness. All who earned less than £160 per annum were to pay fourpence each week into the Insurance Fund, while for each insured worker the employer was to contribute threepence and the Treasury twopence, an arrangement which gave rise to Lloyd George's famous campaign slogan: 'Ninepence for Fourpence'. In return there was to be a guaranteed benefit of ten shillings a week in case of sickness, and free medical attention was to be provided by doctors on the panel system, the panel being the list of insured patients a doctor became responsible for in addition to his private patients. The provisions did not cover the insured worker's family, neither did they extend to the cost of specialist services, hospital treatment, or dental and ophthalmic attention – unless the Approved Society to which he belonged was outstandingly efficiently or humanely run. The objections to the scheme of the private companies were to a large extent met by the setting up of these Approved Societies to administer it; some insurance companies, in fact, became Approved Societies in their own right. But these were purely organs of financial administration; the doctors would not be controlled by them or by local councillors or yet by civil servants, and instead the medical care provisions of the Act were supervised by local Insurance Committees on which the general practitioner was heavily represented.

The Act thus set up a difficult form of administration which was to hamper the growth of a truly national health service until 1948 – and even after. Little attempt was made to link the new medical services to the existing activities of the Local Government Board, and through it, to the Poor Law agencies – although partly because that body had won a reputation for obstruction. Again there was to be no great government spending; insurance, rather than state aid, was to provide the basis for the scheme and the model for the social services in the years to come. Yet insurance, which to Winston Churchill embodied 'the future of democratic politics', and in spite of the criticisms of Beatrice Webb, did indeed provide a striking new departure and went a long way towards reshaping the democratic state [doc. 17]. It demanded a totally new administrative pattern, and it brought a new degree of interference into economic life; it established a new relationship between the worker and his employer quite beyond that of the simple cash wage, and set up a vital new link between citizen and state which would be strong enough eventually, when the insurance foundation of his contract had been shown to be insufficient, for him to be able to base his claim to welfare upon membership of the community alone. For the insurance basis of the Liberal construction was indeed unsound, and would have to be modified; it could never be insurance in the accepted sense of a private contract between a man and a commercial company, for the risks of misfortunes like these could never be assessed on a personal actuarial basis. Its premiums were fixed as the result of political, not financial decisions; its benefits could be boosted or reduced at will by governments who could also move large sums from normal taxation to its support; and such risks as there were were 'pooled risks', in which the more fortunate members of the working class would sustain the less fortunate. While the insurance scheme of the Liberal Government may well be seen as the device called upon and extended by the dying age of individualism to meet sudden and partly unforeseen emergencies, the implications for the future were none the less enormous. It could not endure, but once begun, the onset of mass unemployment and the sharp fall in the value of money would make more effective action on the part of the state essential to ensure subsistence for all regardless of insurance qualifications.

Lloyd George saw clearly that it was merely the beginning; that medical treatment would have to be provided for the families of insured workers, and that widows' and orphans' pensions must follow. He never, for himself, put the Act higher than 'a great social experiment', which made life more bearable for the few without providing a full social provision for the many. He was very much aware of the obstacles to any further advance. "I have joined the Red Cross. I am in the Ambulance Corps. I am engaged to drive a wagon through the twistings and turnings and ruts of the Parliamentary Road" (40). In this spirit, and in the face of such difficulties, were the foundations of the welfare state put down.

THE FIRST WORLD WAR

The outbreak of war in 1914 found the welfare state in its infancy. The Poor Law was still the basis for the treatment of poverty, and unemployment benefits were low and limited in time. Treatment for ill-health, outside the Poor Law, was given to the worker and not to his family, and little was done for hospitals, specialist services or preventive medicine. In the wider sense of welfare, education was compulsory only up to the age of fourteen, and of the 200,000 pupils in secondary schools, only a quarter occupied free places; three million children, of whom many deserved better, were confined to primary education. Housing still lagged behind even basic necessity, and social reform of all kinds was still inhibited by the old *laissez-faire* suspicion of state intervention and still governed by the convenient permissive idea. Palliatives, rather than radical programmes of reform, had been applied (6).

Yet this kind of balance sheet tends to obscure real, if limited, achievement. A need had been recognised by both Majority and Minority Reports of 1909, and important practical steps had been taken towards the concept of the 'national minimum'. The welfare services, especially where they concerned children, were making slow growth, and the framework at least of better secondary education had been provided. The outlines of a new building were faintly evident; the walls would need to be strengthened by later generations, but it was not without foundations, for the Liberals had asserted the vital principles of confiscatory taxation and the supremacy of the Lower House over traditional privilege in the bitter constitutional struggle of 1909-11.

But in the hard fight to establish these principles the Liberal Party went far towards destroying itself. It could not exist after the elections of 1910 without the support of Labour and Irish votes in the House of Commons, and its policies after that date — in Ireland, in social reform, and over the trade unions — became to a significant degree the policies of its allies; and in following them, especially towards the end of Home Rule, the Liberals were led into such deep political difficulties that we are able to discern the disintegration of the Radical Party even before the embarrassments of war and the split of 1916. It had played an indispensable role in the story of the welfare state, for it had broken through the strong walls of privilege; and the torch would be handed on to a Labour Party which to a very large extent the Liberals themselves had nurtured. It was not an easy transition, but in the extension of gradualist welfare reform it is a vital one. The role of the Parliamentary Labour Party before 1914 was a particularly frustrating one. It saw its policies annexed by the Liberals, yet the need to reverse the Osborne Judgment and the crippling burden of the two elections of 1910 ensured that its general support for the Liberals would have to go on; but this in turn provoked a reaction from their rank and file, deflected by syndicalism and the consciousness that the purchasing power of wages was in decline, away from the constitutional policies of their parliamentary leaders towards a dangerous phase of industrial action. The Labour M.P.s, however, soldiered on, and they gained the reward for their support. The Trade Union Act of 1913 and the measure to provide payment for M.P.s set the Labour Party on sure foundations and helped to guide it once more into constitutional channels; for if the Liberal Party had deferred to Labour in these years to the extent of adopting its measures, so had the Labour Party become steeped in liberal parliamentary traditions. The Labour Party thus strengthened and directed was to become a vital factor in the progress of the welfare state; the constitutional manner of its early growth ensured that social reform

33

would continue to be moderate and gradualist, and that the new society would be a modification of the old rather than the radical creation of something quite new.

This development went on during the war, and Labour played a full part in its conduct both at national and shopfloor level. It was impossible to create a truly national Coalition without a Labour leader, Arthur Henderson, in the War Cabinet; and it was equally impossible to mobilise the full resources of the nation without the cooperation of trade union officials at every level. The collapse of the Liberals as a major party left Labour as the radical alternative (the spur to social progress — although far from exclusively its instrument), and the new Constitution of 1918, which opened membership to sympathisers from all classes, and its accompanying moderate programme, *Labour and the New Social Order*, gave it enormous potential.

The cause of social welfare gained much more than this. The progress of reform came virtually to a standstill. Trotsky called war 'the locomotive of history', and just as it accelerated the declining trends already visible in the British economy, so did its interruption of social progress make action necessary afterwards on a very considerable scale in order to recover time lost. Working class losses were painfully clear, in the removal of breadwinners, in inadequate housing, and in wretched conditions of work and education. War revealed yet again the appalling deficiencies in health of those who were medically examined, and exposed the poverty, in a national emergency, of the nation's resources (6). Yet it also made clear what a full use of those resources could create; free trade and *laissez-faire* principles suffered body-blows, and economic controls of all kinds showed what could be achieved by the state in the interests of the community as a whole. It brought, too, a vision of the future, doubtless encouraged, in part, to ensure the full participation of the people; a glimpse that all this effort directed towards destruction could well be used in the building of a better world, in the sense that Fisher introduced his Education Act in 1918 as "a fitting monument of the great impulse which is animating the whole nation during the War". The fulfilment of that promise depended on many things, but particularly on whether Lloyd George could honour his own promises of social reform. But the Radical of 1909 was now the leader of a predominantly Conservative administration, and there had been little shift either in the class structure of the country or in the location of social and economic power. Postwar frustration would lead to a renewal of popular agitation, much more dangerous to the established order in the heavily charged atmosphere of the early 1920s, in which serious economic difficulties would add to the reluctance of the ruling classes to grant effective social reform. The insistent demands from below were linked with political extremism; the reluctance displayed above was coloured by selfishness. The grounds for compromise were lacking, and the community had not yet achieved the balance which the creation of a more just society demanded. The nation, in short, was not yet mature enough to achieve the welfare state.

4   Between the Wars

In the light of the short periods of concentrated social reform before 1914 and after 1945, it would be easy to dismiss these years as ones of very limited progress, with a thin framework of welfare just managing to survive in the face of unprecedented depression. Yet if it is accepted that the period before 1914 had seen a significant move towards the achievement of the 'national minimum', and that the years after 1945 brought the nation very close to the ideal of an optimum in welfare services, then it is probable that the intervening years provide a link between them. Certainly the forces working against genuinely reforming growth were immense; yet it went on, often hidden because it was to a large extent inspired by an impetus towards change which was set up by the momentum of social policy itself as it sought the answers to the questions raised by the problems of its own development. In general outline, the 1920s were years of optimism, slowly fading, and to be abandoned altogether in the economic crisis of 1929-31; the 1930s brought a much more critical examination, sometimes highly pessimistic, of the social deficiencies of the community; and while the Second World War brought once more the fast engine of change, many of the achievements of the late 1940s are rooted in the bitter years before 1939.

THE 'TWENTIES

The education of a nation is never an easy process. The postwar boom was deceptive. The old world had gone for ever, and in the face of steady economic decline and the stripping away of all illusions about the past or the present, Britain had to accept that salvation would come only through her own efforts. Yet it was easier for a war-weary nation to cling to the view that all would one day be well provided that governments practised a strict economy until the terms of trade swung once more in its favour. Such thoughts offered little hope of radical social reform, and this was also limited by the very real apprehension of socialism, to be seen in such fearsome reality in Soviet Russia. The administrations of the period, moreover, would be predominantly Conservative; and while there would be pressure from the Left, the two interwar Labour Governments offered little more than amelioration. The prevailing political philosophy would work against more than a modest use of the resources of the state, and towards reducing the scope of the social services and making them actuarially sound.

This, however, proved to be the most intractable problem of the age, and as the solution was pursued, further instalments of social reform were achieved – an example of how progress in welfare grows to a very marked extent from its own limitations. The insurance principle of 1911 was under intense strain by 1920, making essential those adjustments which would alter radically the accepted view of the financing of the social services. At the end of the war contributions and benefits were brought into line with a cost of living which had doubled during the war; the exemption limit was raised to £250, and by 1920 virtually all workers had been brought into the scheme. In 1921 allowances were increased for those with dependents, and, in spite of the Geddes economies, the scheme was soon hopelessly in debt. For Churchill and Llewellyn Smith had sought merely to deal with temporary unemployment, assuming a rate of no more than 10 per cent; while Beveridge, behind them, believed that their scheme was the first part only of a much wider plan to limit unemployment, and that industries of persistent depression and widespread casual employment should be excluded from it and given special treatment [doc. 18]. Yet by 1922 there were 1.5 million men out of work, and the indiscriminate widening of the scheme in 1920 had meant that a new factor had entered into the formulation of social policy, that of a lasting hard core of unemployed, long out of benefit, who were going to be sustained either from taxes or the contributions of those away from the depressed areas of the basic industries who could look forward to reasonably secure work. While the terminology of insurance was retained, temporary and uncovenanted benefits were paid to those who had exhausted their insurance cover. Twelve measures of this sort were passed by 1927, when 'transitional benefits', as they were called at that time, although cut from 18s to 17s, were paid for an unlimited period and almost without condition.

After 1930 insurance and relief were virtually indistinguishable (22). Thus, while it is important that the recognition grew that the unemployment which marked the interwar years was no longer a personal insurable risk but a national responsibility, in the sense that Beatrice Webb and Beveridge had identified it before 1914, considerable controversy began to develop over whether the community, in affording relief so imprudently, was necessarily acting in the best interests of the nation as a whole. The trade unions, and to some extent the Labour Party, pressed consistently for higher benefits, paid without condition, and as a charge on taxation; but while a policy of virtually indiscriminate relief did achieve certain national ends in helping to keep up the wages of those in work and maintaining the purchasing power of those who were not, there was in opposition to this considerable feeling that such a policy would impose a crushing burden on both public and private enterprise; while the more informed critics maintained that it would absolve government and both sides of industry from any more radical efforts to relieve unemployment by fundamental and necessary reorganisation. Whether assisting the economy in the short run, or damaging it in the long run, the identification of social policy with national needs was becoming very clear indeed, and the crisis of 1931 would bring the whole matter under urgent consideration.

Over the same period, improvements in the health of the nation moved forward sporadically and were achieved with difficulty. The Ministry of Health was set up in 1919, with Christopher Addison in charge, ably assisted by Sir Robert Morant, chief author of the Education Act of 1902, since 1911 Chairman of the National Health Insurance Commission, and yet one more of that dedicated band of public servants who assisted in the slow emergence of a fairer society. The lessons of the war seemed clear. Before it, the resources of the nation had been wasted; of every nine conscripts medically examined after 1916, four were totally discarded and only three were found fit for active military service. But again, in the prevailing political and economic conditions of the time, the path would not be an easy one, and while there were new postwar scales for health insurance as there were for unemployment benefits, nothing was done for dependents and there was little encouragement of positive health. Administration was difficult, for the new Department absorbed the old Local Government Board as well as the Insurance Commissions; and its burdens included public health and housing, the old Poor Law, hospitals and infirmaries. It was a difficult mixture, and its environmental work suffered as a consequence.

A Royal Commission on the Health Service sat between 1924 and 1926. A minority report recommended the abolition of the Approved Societies and the handing over of their tasks to elected local authorities. It also asked for benefits for dependents, treasury grants for the health service, and a much wider range of treatment. 'The ultimate solution will lie in the direction of divorcing the medical service entirely from the insurance system and recognizing it . . . as a service to be supported from the general health funds' (23). While the Majority Report accepted this as an ultimate solution, it judged that the time was not yet ripe, suggesting that the state 'may justifiably turn from searching its conscience to exploring its purse'. It would be difficult to find a phrase which better illustrates the dilemma of the interwar years, the sharp antithesis between the ideal and the possible; yet at the same time one sees again how the shortcomings of a social service itself would eventually provide the incentive towards change.

But both Labour Governments of these years had to explore the public purse with care. Philip Snowden, Chancellor of the Exchequer in 1924, failed to increase the level of Old Age Pensions, although he did raise the limit of exemption on means other than earnings, for the burden of an ageing society was becoming for the first time apparent. Labour was also concerned to show that its leaders could govern as well as those of any other party, and this inevitably led them to govern like the others, concerned above all to balance the budget and preserve the soundness of the economy. It was coming to be a generally accepted view that the level of the social services depended upon the economic health of the nation at large, another sense in which social policy and economic policy were essentially linked. These were ideas which were, of course, much more typical of the Conservative administrations which filled most of the interwar years, and the Baldwin Government of 1924-29 is an excellent example. Baldwin was far from insensitive; he was acutely aware of the moral challenge of Socialism and looked to the reconciliation of the poor, intent on that sort of defensive, but nonetheless vital, reform which has marked British Conservatism. Churchill, back in the party and at the Exchequer, looked to a Peelite policy of recovery and reconstruction in which the people would find greater security. Yet the chances of this were deemed to depend on the reduction of taxation, so that the social policy of Neville Chamberlain at the Ministry of Health had to be built on retrenchment. Chamberlain dominated Conservative social reform; he had some idealism, and he was a first-class administrator, but he had neither the resources nor the imagination to practise generosity. Lloyd George, already moving towards the view that the state would have to play a much more active and dramatic part in generating work and welfare, once said that he had 'a retail mind in a wholesale business'. Beveridge was now advocating an integrated insurance scheme for the whole community; Chamberlain's legislation of 1926 and 1927 was a limited reflection of this. Widows', orphans' and old age pensions were introduced for the first time on a contributory basis; thus, while the range of benefits was extended, it was made clear that they would have to be paid for. In a similar fashion, health benefits were increased and were applied to dependents for the first time, but again contributions went up. A full analysis of the scheme shows how little the Treasury had to bear; finely calculated insurance was to provide the basis for higher basic benefits, and personal thrift would have to account for anything above them. 'The full circle of security for the worker', which Chamberlain sought, was not achieved, and a more direct policy would be necessary. Hugh Dalton, for Labour, pointed out that if taxes had not been reduced, pensions could have been doubled without any higher contributions at all. The question of social and economic priorities was at the heart of the political arguments of these years; and just as the impossibility of extending insurance to cover all the risks of employment was a lesson being slowly and painfully learned, so the pressure on politicians to regard pensions and extended unemployment benefits as a charge on taxation, and to be more imaginative in their development of the full resources of the state, was increased.

In fact, Chamberlain's greatest contribution to reform was an indirect one, that of the reorganisation of local government in 1929, the expression, perhaps, of a long-held Conservative belief, appropriate to a Chamberlain, that social reform was at its most effective at the local level. Fewer and larger authorities were established, and the Poor Law Guardians went, their functions handed over to Public Assistance Committees which were to be supervised by the new county boroughs and county councils. The actual payment of relief was already a matter into which social insurance schemes had intruded; and the new Committees were to deal with demands for help from those whom they did not cover, while the Poor Law hospitals were to be transferred to the Public Health Authorities. The new Committees became responsible for the care of the young, the old, and the mentally sick; but there were no new institutions to put them in, merely those handed over by the Guardians. Thus, from an act of reorganisation, the welfare services of the future could grow; and the realisation that the Poor Law belonged to the past, and that better foundations would be necessary for whatever followed, gave the stimulus to the eventual creation of a truly National Health Service.

THE 'THIRTIES
Yet for all this evolutionary development, it was once more a national disaster, the economic crisis of 1931, which eventually made it clear that a full mobilisation of the national resources, quite beyond the mere payment of relief, would be necessary in order to deal with the social and economic problems it had aggravated. The second Labour Government faced a situation which had brought over 1.5 million unemployed by the spring of 1930. The drain on public resources was immense, and when by 1931 nearly 3 million men were out of work, the insurance fund was in debt by £100 million and local relief was in shreds. More

men were brought into the scope of transitional benefit, and MacDonald was warned that the whole economy was at risk. Advised by his own and by foreign bankers to introduce economies if the foreign loans necessary to balance the budget and save the pound were to be attracted, the Prime Minister found his Cabinet divided, and resigned to form the National Government in 1931. To meet the immediate crisis stringent economy orders were applied; normal benefits were cut by 10 per cent and transitional benefits were paid only after a searching family means test. The bitter depth of the depression had arrived, with its mute misery and hunger marches, and beneath that dreadful bitterness were nurtured the vital attitudes of the postwar years [docs 19, 20].

One was marked by despair. The forces of the Left were again in confusion, and there was an instinctive feeling at their roots that the collapse of their Government had been engineered by powerful financial interests, intent on wrecking an administration that would have survived to succeed. More precise was the growing conviction among intellectuals that the capitalist order had indeed broken down. Beatrice Webb admitted in sorrow that her faith in the possibility of the removal of destitution without a corresponding change in the social and economic order had been misplaced, and she was prepared to declare, as late as 1938, that Marx's predictions had been correct (46). Harold Laski, whose writings and teaching on political theory had enormous influence, maintained consistently that it would be impossible for the working classes to achieve their ends within the framework of parliamentary democracy as it then existed, for it had grown essentially out of middle-class values. This perceptible move towards Marxism among the intellectuals, reflected in the literature of the age, was partly a reaction against the spread of Fascism in Europe; but it was also very much a part of the loathing they felt for an industrial system which could treat humanity with such contempt. Liberal democracy and its concomitant, individual commercial enterprise, seemed in grave danger. That it did not collapse is the result of several factors, of which those concerned with the Second World War, in which it was vindicated, will be examined later; but for our present purposes it is necessary to look once more at that process of adaptation by which it survived, to a large degree by displaying a greater concern for people, to bring a welfare state nearer. The Labour movement shed its extremists once more, and maintained its belief in the amelioration of existing society — and it is significant that one of these extremists, John Strachey, reappeared as a leading member of the reforming Attlee administration in 1945. Enlightened Conservatives, many of whom, like Harold Macmillan, were to be in power after the Second World War, showed compassion and understanding [doc. 19]. The lessons of the 1930s were painful ones; they were absorbed more easily in the war, and they bore fruit in the years immediately following it.

For the moment there was the halting search for a more effective solution of a problem now seen in fuller perspective. Measures for the relief of unemployment were put on a firmer, fairer basis. The most profound lesson of the crisis of 1931 was not that indiscriminate welfare was a strain on the resources of the state, but that the insurance scheme had been submerged beneath a system of careless relief to the ablebodied, largely without the condition of genuinely seeking work, which had discouraged the state, the employers and the trade unions from finding any more effective answer to the problem of distress. These were the views of Beveridge, who provided vital evidence to the Royal Commission of 1932 [doc 18] and (11). It recommended in its Report that a distinction should be drawn between insurance and relief, and that a statutory national body should in future deal with public assistance, thus removing it from the sphere of local politics and lifting the burden from some of the poorer authorities – for one of the ironies of the interwar years was that in the more favoured areas, which could well afford poor relief, there was little for the Public Assistance Committees to do.

The Act of 1934, passed some weeks after the cuts of 1931 had been restored, thus set up two bodies. The Unemployment Insurance Statutory Committee, of which Beveridge was chairman until 1943, was designed to make the insurance plan solvent; it did so by devising a scheme which would break even at an unemployment rate of 16.75 per cent, which was that existing in 1934 and was never reached again, so that it never again ran into debt (8). The Unemployment Assistance Board, which virtually completed the destruction of the old Poor Law, was to bring about a common level of supplementary aid, which was both a significant step towards the national minimum and a confession that in some areas there would be no recovery in the foreseeable future, and that therefore a locally administered scheme of poor relief was inequitable. In order to receive assistance, a worker had to prove that he was willing to find a job and agree to an investigation of his financial position. An unpleasant word came into general use; the 'means test' was bitterly resented by the poor, and their opposition to it delayed the full working of the scheme until 1939. Yet a stabilised insurance scheme and a more positive programme of national relief ensured that the movement towards national welfare would continue on the same broad path as before.

But there were also welcome, if faint, signs that national leaders were realising that it was not enough merely to ease the misery of unemployment, and that it would be necessary to take very real measures to cure it. The National Government moved nearer to the concept of national planning, although by no means as far as the Liberal programmes constructed by Lloyd George and J.M. Keynes would have them go in using the financial resources of the State to create growth and employment. The limits of such programmes are more apparent today than they were in the 1930s, and it is clear that the Government Training Centres for the Unemployed offered no guarantee of work in the end; and the designation as 'special areas' of the old centres of basic industry did little to attract new firms there; and the manipulation of credit was not enough to revive dying staple industries. There was, however, at least, a fuller insight into the truth that social and economic policy could not be separated, and that the former was not a special area of its own, isolated from national policies. In the simplest form of this relationship, it was already evident that unemployment relief could sustain the level of wages and keep up the purchasing power of the people; but there was now a much clearer appreciation of the Beveridge doctrine that social relief had to be accompanied by positive measures to restore full employment, and that there could be no really effective system of state welfare without them. The modified liberalism of men like Beveridge, and a greater inclination to use the resources of the state, would help to weaken political extremism. There was, in any case, a national disinclination to look for extreme and theoretical political solutions. This had made Benthamism and Fabianism peculiarly English growths, and many of the more articulate critics of the age were more concerned with practical and realistic solutions, while the Englishman will readily accept the advice of those who will show him exactly how his condition is to be improved — as the adulation of Beveridge after 1942 showed **(39)**.

An intense social investigation fed on the distress of the 1930s, as Booth had applied himself to that of the 1890s. Rowntree surveyed York again and found that the lot of the very poor had changed but little: Boyd Orr went on with his life's work on the problems of nutrition: the non-political P.E.P. produced one damning report after another. More evidence emerged of a fragmented community, but the divisions were now more subtle and more intriguing; for while there is a good deal of evidence, perhaps surprising, that for most of the people living standards rose slightly over these years, for the rest there was bare survival, with little escape from the tyranny of destitution. Evidence multiplied that the root causes of this destitution were more than old age and unemployment; they were related also to the possession of large families by those in work. In this identification of the more specialised

areas of real poverty by much more precise methods of social investigation was the growing awareness that the differential between the low
wage earners with large families and those who were unemployed and in
receipt of benefit was very small indeed [doc. 20]. This in turn gave rise
to a new campaign, that for family allowances, or social relief for those
in work, which was so ably led by Eleanor Rathbone until its successful
conclusion in 1945. Deficiencies in health were also thus revealed, and
they were made even more obvious by documents like the P.E.P. report
on the British health services of 1937. An unnecessarily complex
administration in which health, in the words of the White Paper of
1944, was 'many people's business but nobody's full responsibility' (14),
produced insufficient hospitals, a thoroughly inadequate housing
provision, a grossly high rate of infant mortality and a very low standard
of health among children generally. Once more the conscience of the
nation was being aroused; if the State had to plan its resources better,
then so had its people to find a new unity, a new sense of caring for
each other; perhaps one of the most striking features of these years is
the resurgence of the voluntary services and societies whose work had
been invaluable in the nineteenth century, and which were now shedding
some of the reactionary associations they appeared to have before 1914.
They revived in close partnership with the state, a link fostered by the
National Council for Social Service, and played a vital part in meeting
the needs of the expectant and nursing mother, the handicapped, and
especially the blind.

It was in these years also that the social services were beginning to
extend more effectively beyond the fields of health and poverty. It had
taken precisely a hundred years for a new industrial society, after 1834,
to get rid of all the old assumptions about the relief of destitution, and
to treat it as a national responsibility. There was an equally slow
awakening in the spheres of environmental health and education.
Housing policy only emerged as a public service after the First World
War, when the Addison Act enjoined local authorities to lease newly
built houses and to fix the rents in accordance with the tenant's
capacity to pay, any loss to the authority in excess of a penny rate
being made good by the Exchequer. But it did little for the very poor —
here, once more, this new division in society — and in the atmosphere of
the early 1920s its demands on the public purse became unpopular. It
was abandoned in 1923 when Neville Chamberlain limited Exchequer
grants and encouraged private enterprise to build more houses for sale.
The same principle entered this field as affected arguments about cash
benefits at this time, and by the Wheatley Act of 1924, the first
Labour Government's most effective domestic measure, the process

was reversed; houses for the poor began to go up in some numbers, although just how few in relation to real need was revealed by the census figures of 1931. The Act of 1924 is important in that it finally put the responsibility for low-priced housing into the court of local government and created a long-term programme by which it could expand.

The National Government modified it in 1933, feeling that with falling costs needs could again be met by the private builder. Slum clearance began in earnest in 1930, under the Labour Government; it was carried on by the National Government, and while half the recognised slums had been destroyed by 1939, much less had been done towards rehousing. New private housing estates grew like mushrooms, many of them scarring the landscape, and a third of the houses on them were within the reach of the better-off worker: there were, in fact, for those who could buy, more houses than were needed, with some builders offering to furnish them free, but for the very poor there were by no means enough, thus providing another example of the divided society of the 1930s. Overall planning, in this, as in other spheres, moved slowly. The Town and Country Planning Act of 1932 bore the old defects of permissive legislation, and while there were a few good examples of fine local, and often private, residential development like that in Welwyn Garden City, evidence of effective planning had to wait for the Barlow Report of 1940 and the blitz.

In education, too, there were faint signs of a more generous society. The provisions of the Fisher Act of 1918 were lost in postwar retrenchment, but its aspirations towards better further education remained a challenge on the statute book. The Hadow Report of 1926 foreshadowed the reorganisation of education which emerged in the Butler Act of 1944. It advocated secondary education for all children, with grammar school places for those with the ability to benefit from them, regardless of need. The Spens Report of 1938 drew attention to the need for technical education, and thus added another element to that tripartite division which was to begin after the war. In this field, perhaps, is the strongest evidence of the combination of personal and national need, for while a full education was deemed to be more and more necessary to individual fulfilment, the nation was at the same time clearly wasting its resources, and delaying the emergence of gifted children from poor families into areas in which they would be able to sustain the much-needed social and economic recovery of the nation — a need which war would reinforce absolutely.

The seeds of a new society thus germinated slowly, but they were watered in a generally favourable intellectual climate. The 'bitter society', as it has been called, produced those who despaired and those who would have destroyed it; but it also brought forward able and sensitive men who still accepted its essential values but who were determined to play their part in ensuring that they did not become a mockery. Labour politicians gave form in the postwar period to the aspirations they had developed in the years before it [doc. 26], and those years also produced a generation of Conservatives whose attitudes after 1945 would be crucial [doc. 19]. It produced a whole generation prepared to accept as axiomatic the doctrines of Keynes that planning in a free society was not only possible but would be fruitful – a whole consensus, in fact, of future influential leadership. The vast output of critical writing on a whole range of subjects over these years had a marked effect on the development of those who, young and perhaps revolutionary in the 1930s, found a new identity with the community during the war, and played a large part in the selection of the reforming Government of 1945. The humane influence of writers like J.B. Priestley, on the other hand, found a wider and less rarifed response among countless men of good will. William Temple brought the Church of England firmly into the political arena, and humanitarianism of a new kind brought the Pilgrim Trust into being; its very influential *Men Without Work,* published in 1938, provided an exhaustive and thought-provoking survey of the whole problem of unemployment, particularly in its social and 'hereditary' aspects [doc. 20]. There was a pervading sense of unfeeling neglect and criminal division; even the realisation, by 1939, that the nation which had so far failed to stand firm in the face of the obscenity of Nazi Germany had perhaps done so little because its social and economic values were out of joint, and its community structure weak. The spirit of Dunkirk would go far to remedy both.

5 The Modern Welfare State

THE TESTING OF THE NATION, 1939-45

The first great war of the twentieth century inspired dreams of social change which faded in the complacency and depression of the interwar years. The second brought a promise that was sustained. Both brought a necessary and greater concern for the ordinary people: both forced governments to assume heavier responsibilities for their welfare: both brought a better use of the nation's resources (6). But after 1945 there was a much greater awareness of past inadequacies, a much greater shock to national complacency, and an even greater realisation of the transition to come. There was also a greater political maturity, much of it learned in the sufferings of the 1930s, and a new social cohesion brought about by an equality of sacrifice and suffering. Britain was the only nation state which went through the war from beginning to end to emerge victorious without marked political or social disturbance, and this fundamental stability made it possible for her to get on with the task of making society more equitable even while the war went on – although it would also ensure that its foundations would remain largely unchanged. What is more, the provision of the hope of this reconstructed community – which today we call the welfare state – became the essential requisite for the total participation in war of all its members, and a good deal of the national war effort was directed to the purpose of remedying the deficiencies of the past. Churchill was anxious lest public discussion about the Beveridge Report should take attention away from the task of winning the war [doc. 25]. It was, in fact, a part of it.

This new vision of the future was first concentrated upon the nation's children. The evacuation of so many of them from the threatened cities to the countryside did much to bring the two nations of the 1930s together. The still wretched conditions of the towns and the poverty of family life were revealed, and *The Economist* called it 'the most important subject in the social history of the war'. It undoubtedly prepared the way for the development of the family welfare services [doc. 21]. Free milk came, dramatically, barely a week after Dunkirk – that symbol at once of the past shortcomings of the nation and of its determination to rebuild [doc. 22]. Free immunisation followed, and in 1941 came the first free issue of cod-liver oil, with the words: 'the raw material of the race is too valuable to be put at risk', and the provision of a heavily subsidised and comprehensive school meals service. What is of equal importance is that most of these services were available to all, regardless of means, and thus marked an important step away from the past and into the future.

Supplementary pensions for the old came for the first time in 1940. The welfare of the workers, especially those on low incomes, was improved; food prices were stabilised in 1940, and in 1941 further steps were taken to hold down the cost of living, that vital general factor in the welfare of the aged and the poor [doc. 27]. In the same year, the hated family means test was abolished, and the provision of welfare moved slowly but significantly in the direction of being based on needs rather than on means. Of as much importance to the welfare of the nation was that the powers of the State were strengthened. While Churchill, the Service Ministers and the Chiefs of Staff were at the apex of the wartime administration, a vital place was occupied, not far below, by Sir John Anderson and his Lord President's Committee. Its function, in bringing together economic and domestic policy, fulfilled what had before been only fitfully glimpsed, and brought full realisation of what a benevolent state could achieve when it had the will.

The economy was managed as never before; production was co-ordinated, and, more important, full employment was maintained, thus giving the Beveridge doctrine a vital reality. Coordinated research brought a national dividend, and the people as a whole, in spite of war-time shortages, had never been better fed. Here the role of the Ministry of Food was crucial, and many of the deficiencies in the diet of the working people especially were eliminated. In health, the development of penicillin and the sulphonamides, and vast improvements in operative techniques, brought immense benefit to the serviceman, yet they also stressed the shortcomings of the prewar health service, and showed what could be done for all. A Ministry of Health statement in 1941 insisted that there could be no return to the old situation of unrelated hospital units; and the White Paper of 1944 accepted the principle of a free and comprehensive health service (14).

Rationing, shared hardships and shortages brought a new community sense; its reality has been questioned, but its influence certainly endured into the postwar world. Planning is one thing; the willing cooperation of the people is another; and the development of true welfare depends on both. Countless observers, particularly those from the United States, saw a new eagerness to serve and a new spirit of comradeship; Lord

Woolton, who fed the nation with efficiency and humour, spoke of a moral as well as an economic revolution. At the same time, the most certain guarantee of a welfare society after the war was in the presence of a large number of Labour ministers in the Coalition Government. Attlee, as Churchill's deputy, proved an able chairman and administrator: Arthur Greenwood was given responsibility for postwar reconstruction: and in the planning and utilisation of the nation's resources of manpower the mighty Ernest Bevin, recruited direct from his leadership of the Transport and General Workers' Union, played a part in the conduct of the war second only to that of Churchill, and in doing so he ensured that the people he was forced to direct were going to be adequately looked after. He persuaded Churchill to insert into the Atlantic Charter of 1942, a statement of the war and peace aims of the two allies issued jointly with President Roosevelt, the vital fifth clause: 'They desire to bring about the fullest collaboration between all nations in the economic field, with the object of seeing for all improved labour standards, economic advance and social security.'

Labour gained as much, however, from the fact that below the surface of public affairs, where a party truce obtained, its supporters went on with their political activities. Conferences were held and new policies were put forward, often reaching beyond the cautious White Papers issued by the Coalition Government, and much more precise than the policies Labour had itself advocated down to 1940. One of the remarkable effects of the war was the seemingly insatiable demand it brought for serious discussion, much of it political and social. The BBC Brains Trust, begun diffidently by the Corporation, became the forum of the nation: paperbacks, full of serious content, became of age, and sold for mere coppers in wartime economy editions: service education classes like those sponsored by the Army Bureau of Current Affairs produced an overwhelming impression of a wide interest in political and philosophical matters. With this enormous interest in the reconstructed society the future would bring, it was inevitable that past deficiencies should be condemned, and that the political leaders of the interwar years should be charged with having failed to produce a nation militarily and socially fit for the great test that was forced upon it. Politically, as the war ended, the stirrings were leftwards. Sir Richard Acland's Commonwealth Party broke the party truce in 1943 and won significant ground with radical policies; and perhaps the most influential political tract of the war was Michael Foot's *Guilty Men,* part of Victor Gollancz's consistent attack on the policies of the years before the war. In vain did anonymous Tories go into print to resist this tide; to the perceptive few, the Labour landslide of 1945 came as no surprise. If the British people came of age in the war, it was perhaps most evident in the sense that they were determined to exercise the right of choice; and that, in itself, would indicate political change (8).

THE FOUNDATIONS OF THE FUTURE

In June 1941 Arthur Greenwood informed the House of Commons that an Inter-Departmental Committee had been appointed to examine the existing range of social insurance and to make recommendations for the future, and that its chairman would be Sir William Beveridge. By November 1942 its report had been completed; it was signed by Beveridge alone, since it was not felt to be appropriate to add the names of the civil servants who had helped him to produce a document which was bound to provoke some discussion of policy. When, in fact, in December, it went on sale to the public, the debate over what came simply to be known as the Beveridge Report was far more animated than anyone could have foreseen (12).

It recommended, in unexciting terms, the extension and integration of schemes already in existence in order to provide insurance against loss of earning power through the hazards of sickness, unemployment and old age, and suggested a guaranteed income at subsistence level — that is, enough to secure the bare necessities of life, such as food, clothing, housing and so on — in all circumstances. In essence, it implied a fundamental departure, for it did not advocate relief of specific hardships on a separate basis, as in the past, but sought to provide for the loss of income which any of these misfortunes could bring. There would be very few exceptions, for the other really novel principle of the Beveridge Report was that contained in the element of compulsion and universality; all would pay, and benefits would go to all citizens, regardless of income without stigma or test of means. The benefits envisaged were for unemployment, which would be paid indefinitely provided that the recipient was prepared for retraining after a certain period: widows', retirement, and old age pensions: payments for industrial injury, disablement, and upon death: and, although these were never accepted, for marriage, for deserted wives and for home helps in case of sickness. There would, in short, be the provision of the long-awaited national minimum without a social revolution. Beveridge, that key figure in the making of the British Welfare State, had Liberal origins; he insisted on the principle of insurance to gain subsistence, and he believed that the state should give every encouragement to the private saving that would augment it. It was to him a natural development from the past; he called it a 'British revolution', and he did not envisage any increase in government expenditure.

The importance of the Report was less in its proposals than in its background and assumptions. Behind its enthusiastic reception was the expectation of a nation, reflected in Beveridge's conclusion that 'statement of a reconstruction policy by a nation at war is a statement of the uses to which that nation means to put victory when victory is achieved', and in its very universality, and the insistence on the citizen's claim to benefit 'as of right', there is the strong suggestion that this claim rested less on a contractual insurance obligation than on membership of society itself. But want was not all; and in one of the few heightened passages of the Report Beveridge named it as only one of the 'five giants' which barred the entrance to a better society, the others being disease, ignorance, squalor and idleness. Thus, educational and environmental advance were assumed: so was the provision of a comprehensive health service, built also on insurance and welded into the scheme as a whole: and family allowances, in order to keep at subsistence level the incomes of those who were at work: and a policy of full employment without which, as he had consistently maintained, social measures were mere palliatives (22). There would always be those unfortunates who would need special benefits of the National Assistance type; but Beveridge believed that the more appropriate role for the state, and the proper target for its spending, was in the creation of full employment. A wider social policy was thus a clear and logical development from his programme, in which he crystallised the lessons of the interwar years. There was also to be a greater degree of integration in the social services, for he also recommended the setting up of a new government department to achieve it, calling it tentatively a 'Ministry of Social Security', Before, Britain had possessed the pieces of a social policy, isolated and incomplete; but if the Report was to be accepted they would take on an identity of their own. This impulse towards the integration of the social services, together with the universality and comprehensiveness which implied the willing participation of the whole community, affords the first clear outline of what would become the welfare state.

Its reception, in the depths of war and long before the certainty of victory, ensured that it would be borne along the road to realisation by the new spirit of the nation. The British people, for some time sensing, not clearly, what was wrong with their society, now knew in detail what it was they wanted. Churchill's response was guarded; he did not wish for a diversion from the war effort, and knew full well how Lloyd George's reputation had suffered from the failure to carry out his wartime promises, and as late as 1944 the Coalition Government's own White Paper on Social Insurance carried the warning that welfare was in itself no substitute for productivity [doc. 25] (15). In spite of the misgivings of Ernest Bevin, who believed that the bargaining powers of the trade unions would be weaker in a welfare society, and that man 'could not live by Beveridge alone' — thus supporting the view that true welfare depends on smoothing the rough edges on both sides of industry — Labour wanted the full and immediate application of its proposals; the parliamentary party annexed it, with Sydney Silverman claiming that it represented the basic programme of his party [**doc. 23**]. *The Times* welcomed it: the Liberal Party called it momentous: and a group of young Conservatives, in the long debate of February 1943, tabled a motion calling on the Government to set up the Ministry of Social Security without delay. Postwar attitudes were thus already being determined, and while those of Labour politicians were predictable, the sympathy of those who would in future lead the Conservative Party prepared the way for a bilateral acceptance of the basic principles of reconstruction. The bitter experiences of the years before the war, and the spirit produced by war itself, ensured that there would be little public acrimony; and Beveridge's vital contribution to this was in showing that want and hardship could be removed, and the national minimum established, without extreme measures. His Report is thus part of the tradition of gradualist reform from which the welfare state has descended. He always insisted, in fact, that it was not politics but plain common sense.

But this does not mean that there would be no controversy, and the elaboration of the Beveridge proposals produced the seeds of arguments which have marked the development of the social services since the war. In this respect, three vital assumptions of the Report merit closer examination. First, the principle of universality could never be based on true insurance, and it opened the way to a new dimension of welfare which would be difficult to sustain. Universal coverage seemed appropriate to the mood of a people engaged in common sacrifice, and it would destroy the hated means test. Yet in this radically widened form of social insurance, in which one single contribution was to open the door to a number of assorted benefits, there could be no fine calculation of entitlement on the normal insurance basis of individual contract; there was instead to be a 'pooling of risks', which were to be borne collectively by society, in which, for example, the perennially healthy would bear the burden of the chronic sick, and in which right to benefit derived mainly from membership of a community. In this compulsion, in the elimination of discrimination and in the new social foundation of welfare, we are moving towards a more organic conception of the state. There was bound to be a reaction; comprehensiveness would be resented, both on political grounds and because growing affluence would give some the means of making social provision on their own account; while even in 1943 it was pointed out that the extension of benefits above the working class would, by diluting welfare, make it more difficult to locate and treat real want; and there would be many to argue that the whole conception of a means test was already out-of-date, for while 'means' were easy to estimate and scale, 'needs' required a much more precise measurement and more exact care. All this would weaken the idea of universality, and the concept of a social state which had a collective identity on its own.

Second, Beveridge's plea was that contributions and benefits should be at the same flat rate for all, with benefits fixed at subsistence level. The state had a social duty to enforce an absolute minimum income necessary for subsistence; but to compel people to pay more than was necessary to achieve this level would be an infringement of liberty. Benefits, therefore, would be subsistence ones at the same flat rate for all, and, since the insurance principle was to be at the base of the scheme, this would also imply flat-rate contributions. The idea of subsistence was a marked advance on the attitude of the interwar years, according to which benefits were intended merely to augment other resources — which all too often did not exist. Beveridge called for an adequate income; and while he did anticipate some form of supplementary assistance, he did not expect that a person should be forced to claim it because his insurance benefits were not enough; it was there simply for the anomalies and the misfits. Yet at the same time, the quest for subsistence was to provide the basis for one of the greatest problems in the social schemes of the future, and was to prove in the end to be an unattainable ideal. For it was impossible to determine with precision.

Beveridge suggested a 25 per cent increase on the 1938 level of subsistence indicated by surveys like that of Rowntree; but this, for the latter, had been no more than a convenient sociological line, whereas subsistence level for Beveridge purposes would have to be broad enough to allow for all kinds of economic changes. Money values will fall, price levels will fluctuate, and rents, especially, will show wide variations from area to area, so that the fixing of a truly universal level becomes impossible. If subsistence levels are put high enough to cover all these eventualities, then their related flat-rate contributions will be more than most members of society can afford. Thus, the White Paper of 1944 rejected this aspect of the Beveridge proposals on these very grounds, and while the postwar Labour Government accepted it nominally and tried to achieve it, it was forced more and more to make up the incomes of those who fell below it from National Assistance **(15)**. Beveridge, from the House of Lords, denounced them for abandoning the principle of 'security against want without a means test'; but short of more effective measures against inflation there was little that any postwar Government could have done, although Sydney Silverman and others asked for a more rigidly managed economy [**doc. 27**]. Progressively, the social policies of both major parties would be led towards insurance schemes which provided earnings-related benefits and away from the subsistence principle, and thus open the way to the great pensions controversies of the 1960s.

Beveridge's third guiding principle was that benefits should be added to by voluntary saving formally encouraged by the state, using the Approved Societies to issue additional policies. This was not taken up, with the result that the balance of the plan was distorted — for voluntary saving was meant to supplement the social insurance which would cover basic needs and the national assistance which would deal with special cases. With the shortcomings of the first two, the latter became more important than Beveridge would have wished; and the National Assistance Board of 1948 was the formal result.

If the postwar development of the welfare state, however, was not entirely according to the lines laid down by Beveridge, his Report did provide the main highway to the future, and the broad framework of the Labour achievements of 1945-50. If it sought to provide the means of putting to death those five giants of the past, the difficulties of implementing fully its basic assumptions would provide the basis for the refinements and qualifications of the future.

Yet it was not the only signpost to the postwar world, although the discussion it aroused without doubt gave impetus to the flow of Government White Papers and reports which followed. The White Paper on Social Insurance of 1944 accepted the outlines of the Beveridge Report while questioning its acceptance of subsistence, and tackled the subject without its assumptions (**15**). In 1944, however, the White Paper on Employment Policy made the most far reaching proposal of all the wartime documents by committing the three Coalition parties to a policy of full employment, to be achieved through national spending, public works and state controls. Beveridge, who had hoped that he would have been asked to produce the report on what was the most essential of his assumptions, was already working on his own document, *Full Employment in a Free Society*; when it was published it contained the charge that the official publication had not fully appreciated the weaknesses of the prewar economy or the radical measures that would be necessary to create full employment. Both, however, owed much to the work of Keynes, and while the Labour Government of 1945 tended to follow Beveridge, the assumptions in both marked a striking advance. The White

Paper on a National Health Service accepted the principle of a free and comprehensive health service, yet without any precise recommendations about the contentious issues of administration or the role of the doctors within it **(14)**. The Barlow Report of 1940 and the Scott and Uthwatt Reports of 1942 which stemmed from it, although far from radical in their suggestions, provided the seeds of further growth in the utilisation of land, in planning, and in housing. The White Paper on Educational Reconstruction of 1943, announced that future policy would be based on the assumption that education was a continuing process from primary school to university, and that secondary education would be provided for all **(13)**.

Yet not all was planning. There was also practical achievement. In 1943 a Bill to set up the ministry Beveridge had suggested was carried, and although there was a long-drawn-out quibble over the name, by the end of the war a Ministry of National — not Social — Insurance had been established. In 1943, in spite of the Government's apparent indifference to the land and housing reports, a Ministry of Town and Country Planning was set up, and one of its first documents was the Abercromby *Greater London Plan* of 1944, which, among other things, recommended the setting up of 'New Towns' to deal with the growing congestion of the capital. Town and Country Planning Acts in the next months gave the new department powers over both land yet undeveloped and that which had been planned badly. Housing policy, even more vital after the air raids, was reviewed in 1944, when it was estimated that over a million new homes would be needed. £150 million was allocated to the building of temporary houses, and skilled men were given early release from the forces. The policy of subsidies was reaffirmed, and in order to avoid the embarrassments of 1920, there was to be continuing control over the price of building materials.

Education provided the greatest single achievement of the Coalition Government in domestic affairs, perhaps because it was less radical than other measures in demand, perhaps also because it was directed by one of the most able and enlightened of modern Conservatives, R.A. Butler. The White Paper of 1943 was almost totally embodied in the Education Act of 1944. In it, secondary education for all was laid down; yet it was to be diversified to the extent that at the age of eleven all children would take an examination which would determine their fitness for 'grammar' or 'modern' development, with, sometimes, the opportunity for more specialised technical education. The unreliability of this comparatively early test and the disparity in the quality of education offered in the various types of secondary schools have given rise to the controversies of our own day, now almost laid to rest; but in 1944,

55

although the Act reflected the educational thinking of some twenty years before, its provision of opportunity for secondary education to countless children who had previously been denied it because of lack of parental means, seemed an enormous step forward. There was no thought, however, of using educational policies as instruments of social change, as some extreme reformers wished. The Education Act of 1944, for all the defects that have become obvious with the passing of the years, seemed to offer, more than any other legislation of the war, the best guarantee of the new opportunities the British people sought. It also indicated that the society which afforded those opportunities would not suffer any radical change.

LABOUR'S HARVEST

The Third Labour Government won 393 seats in the 1945 House of Commons, and a huge majority that was sustained by a popular vote of nearly 12 million. The Conservatives and their supporters, in spite of their domination of a war administration which had sponsored the Beveridge Report, issued a number of vital documents on social and economic matters, created a new Insurance Ministry, and introduced family allowances and a vital Education Act, won only 213 seats. The result of the election had clearly been influenced less by admiration of the war policies of a great leader than by the ardent desire for postwar reform, and by the feeling that the prewar record of the Conservatives gave little evidence that they could achieve it. When the new House met on 15 August, the mood of the Government supporters was exultant; a new social system was about to be born, and the promise of the Labour Movement fulfilled; Hugh Dalton spoke of 'walking with destiny' (4). Labour, with its leaders braced by sound experience in war government, and with little apparent responsibility for the conditions which had existed before it, was ideally placed to ride high on the emotions that war had inspired, and to annex and develop the social planning of the administration of which they had been a part.

This had served to sharpen the aims of a party which up to the war had been vague. The omens for their application were good; a plan of demobilisation which was generally accepted as fair had begun; war had brought both the assumption and the reality of full employment; and it had left behind a legacy of administrative control and planning which could easily be invoked in the cause of social and economic reconstruction. There were, however, huge limiting factors beneath; the war had been prodigal of human and material resources; it had brought debts and financial dislocation; full employment would create wage demands and inflation that would, in time, pose as great a threat to the social services as prewar niggardliness, and it masked the fact that nearly half the nation's population was still involved either in the services or in the war industries, and that only 10 per cent of them were creating capital equipment and providing goods for export. On these, since the country had sold over £1,000 million of overseas investments, the future wealth of the community would depend. £3,000 million was still owed to the United States at the end of the war, and the extension of American aid, after the termination of Lend-Lease in 1945, was accompanied by difficult conditions, such as the demand that the pound be restored to full convertibility and that imperial preferences should go. The return to convertibility in 1947 led to a financial crisis in which sterling came under severe pressure, while the full recovery of the economy was continually undermined by the failures of the two pillars which should have sustained it - the railway industry was run down, and the mines, especially in the bitter winter of 1946-47, were not equal to the task of supplying the power the nation needed.

The promise of the Labour Government would also be limited by the demands of a war economy, for the war in the Far East had not ended when it came to power, and it would be faced throughout with the 'cold war', culminating in the stress of fulfilling its obligations in Korea, and it would also be inhibited by the ever-present threat of rising prices. The full development of the welfare state would be constricted by those two great millstones, war and inflation, and the postwar Labour Governments experienced both. They were also faced with the necessity of urgent and piecemeal economic reform. For they dared not, in the desperate postwar situation, attempt to alter radically the economic structure of society, or to introduce positive measures towards social equality. Their chosen course was to further the export drive and increase the productive capacity of the nation, in the attempt to rebuild a broken economy and pull clear of debt. Their policy was built on expediency; they nationalised only about 20 per cent of industry, and only that part of it which had run down to the point where only vast public investment could save it, and incurring, in the case of coal and transport, huge payments of compensation to former shareholders which would burden the full development of those industries in particular and of the economy in general. There was thus only a half-hearted use of the powers of the state; and the concentration upon the export drive revived once more the old antithesis between the claims of productivity on the one hand and the demands of state-provided welfare on the other.

Thus, without Socialism, there would again be compromise. There would be no overall planning of the resources of the state, in which poverty would naturally disappear; and the fundamental liberalism and moderation of Labour's leaders would tend to make the welfare state an extension and modification of what already existed, easing the stresses of a continuing capitalist society [doc. 26]. The people, moreover, resentful of wartime control, would lose the communal spirit of the war, and move towards a greater individualism in which they would tend less to look upon the state as the great provider, regarding its benefits as the provision of the bare minimum on which they themselves could improve. The Labour ministers, still tied to *ad hoc* policies by the growing economic crisis which brought on devaluation in 1949 and defeat in 1951, ceased to bear the look of men who would transform society. But in those early years after 1945 there was still enough idealism, both in them and in the nation, to foster the greatest contribution ever to the building of the welfare state; and while the spirit of those years became dimmed, most of its fundamental assumptions would remain.

Social reconstruction began with the introduction of the Industrial Injuries Bill; benefits for these were in future to be financed by weekly contributions from employers and workers, higher than for sickness, with an industrial pension for those who would never work again. This measure became law in July 1946. By then, the National Insurance Bill had been given a second reading; in the course of the debate its sponsor, James Griffiths, had called up the shades of Keir Hardie, Asquith and Lloyd George, and the Prime Minister stressed the universality of the new services, of their debt to Beveridge, and of the integration of social policy in the wider economic life of the nation [docs 26, 27]. While family allowances were to be a direct charge on taxation, other benefits were to be related to insurance; one single deduction from earnings, with the contribution from the employer, was to be recorded on a stamped card, and it would give entitlement to a variety of benefits – pensions, unemployment, health and sickness. The total sum was to be collected by the Ministry of National Insurance, which would pass on the appropriate portion to the Ministry of Health.

Two considerations recur. First, while yet again it was easy to use the phraseology of insurance, it was now generally recognised that its part in the new scheme would be limited. Arthur Greenwood, during the Beveridge debate of February 1943, had insisted that mass unemployment was a national economic problem and a national responsibility. Even further back, in 1942, the White Paper on Social Insurance, had made it clear that insurance could not cover family allowances or National Assistance, that its part in financing the National Health Service would be a very small one, and forecast that by 1962, 64 per cent of the service's cost would be borne by the Exchequer. Second, the core of the Beveridge Report had ·been the assumption that cash benefits would be paid on a subsistence basis, calculated on 1938 prices with an addition of 25 per cent. The White Paper of 1944 had questioned this, and the Act of 1946 set out merely to provide a 'reasonable insurance' against want, clearly accepting that if flat-rate benefits were set too high, then contributions would be too expensive for the mass of the people. Thus the national minimum had not yet arrived, and those who found that benefits, with inevitable inflation, had fallen below subsistence level, would be driven to the National Assistance Board. While this was created in 1948 with a dramatic flourish that pronounced the old Poor Law dead, its benefits were still to be subject to a personal means test. Beveridge, from the House of Lords, was strongly critical of this abandonment of his basic theme.

Yet in spite of the means test, the National Assistance Board did provide a decisive break with the past. Relief in money terms, over and above insurance, was totally transferred to a national body, from rates to taxes; and it brought to an end that long tradition of welfare — which reached back to Elizabeth I, through the Act of 1929 and the Poor Law of 1834 — that poverty was a matter for local administration and that the poor were the concern of their immediate neighbours; and, since it separated cash benefits from personal services, it opened the way for the development of the local welfare provision, which, since money was not involved, could be offered without hint of charity or pauperism — though the recommendations of the Seebohm Report and the legislation which followed it inaugurated a move back towards local services equipped once more with the power to grant money benefits [doc. 28].

The creation of the National Health Service in 1948 provided the other great pillar of the postwar welfare state; it was of even greater significance since it reached nearer to the heart of the debate on the social services. Before the war, a far from adequate health service had been available only to those who qualified by reason of their insurance contract. It did not extend to their dependants, and while the income limit had been raised to £420 per annum in 1942, only half the population had by then been covered. The question of cost, therefore, would be vital to the provision of a comprehensive service, for the existing scheme did not include hospital or specialist treatment, nor did it make freely available dental or ophthalmic services. There was at the same time little central coordination. Doctors were spread all over the country with little relation to real need. There were over 1,200 voluntary hospitals of varying efficiency, and some 1,500 more had been developed by local authorities, from a few good ones to those which had developed from the sick wards of old workhouses. Public health authorities, hospitals, and general practitioners all enjoyed separate administration, as did factory doctors and those employed in the school medical service. Preventive and curative medicines were hopelessly mixed, and supervisory functions were charged to such diverse bodies as the Ministry of Health, the Ministry of Education, local authorities, the factory inspectorate, and the Poor Law administration. The time had come for a complete replanning of the nation's health resources.

As far back as 1924 the Minority Report on health provision had looked to the creation of a truly national service, and the Beveridge Report of 1942 had assumed that it would be universal. It fell to Aneurin Bevan, the Labour Minister of Health, to bring order from this chaos, to deal with the problems of cost, of administration, and of the traditional individualism and conservatism of the medical profession, the latter task far from easy for one long identified with the left wing of the Labour movement, and whose Socialism was deeprooted in the desperate conditions of the Welsh valleys in which he had first gone to work. He proved to be an outstanding administrator, and, in private negotiation, possessing the tact and diplomacy which eventually produced the National Health Service which exists to this day.

The question of cost was the easiest to dispose of, for this was a political decision, and Bevan let it be known that nothing would be allowed to stand in the way of making good health services available to all regardless of income. Costs might have been cut by retaining the principle of the upper income limit for full membership; but the minister would not contemplate a 'two-tier service', making it instead all-inclusive and compulsory, the essential feature, again, of postwar Labour legislation. There was little opposition on the other side of the House, for it was clearly what the people wanted **(4)**.

The organisation of such a service proved to be vastly more difficult. It was to be completely in the hands of the Ministry of Health, with the Minister responsible to Parliament for its administration: a Central Health Services Council, to consist largely of representatives of the medical bodies, was to advise him on the conduct and development of the service. Beneath, there was to be a tripartite administration. First, local authorities were to look after preventive health and the environ-mental services, with Medical Officers of Health exercising much the same functions as before. Second, the administration of hospital and specialist services was to be supervised by twenty Regional Hospital Groups: each was to have its own Hospital Board, appointed by the Minister from members of local health authorities, from the universities and from medical associations, and was to be responsible for the conduct and planning of the hospital services for the region: these would appoint voluntary Hospital Management Committees to be responsible for the normal running of single hospitals or small groups of hospitals: while the teaching hospitals were to be administered separately by their own governing bodies, appointed by the Minister from members of the Regional Boards, from the specialists who worked in them, and from members of the universities concerned.

But it was the third aspect of administration, concerned with general practice, which in the end gave Bevan his greatest difficulty, and it involved him in a long and wearing struggle with the doctors, during which the concessions he made brought him under the crossfire of the Socialist Medical Association, strongly in favour of the elimination of private practice altogether and the substitution of a state-salaried medical service. Yet there was respect on both sides, for both parties at root were concerned at the standard of the nation's health, and the bitterest polemic was in fact reserved for the political platform and BMA meetings. At the negotiating table, Bevan was fully aware of the need to win the consent of a powerful profession which held the future of the National Health Service in its hands, and slowly convinced it that he had no intention of forcing the doctors into a bureaucratic system that would stifle initiative and damage their relationship with their patients. They would be free to enter or stay out, and to take private patients as they wished; while the patients themselves would be free to take all, or part, or none of the state services offered, and to choose their doctors as they wished.

Bevan proposed that the work of the general practitioners should be supervised by Executive Councils appointed for each county and county borough: each was to consist of twenty-four members, twelve lay and twelve professional; of the professional members seven would represent the doctors, three the dentists, and two the pharmaceutical services. The chairman of each committee was to be appointed by the Minister, and it would be responsible both for the administration of the local health services and for the payment of doctors, dentists, opticians and chemists from a central pool. Two Medical Practices Committees were to be set up, one for England and Wales and one for Scotland. Their task was to ensure the adequate nationwide provision of doctors by controlling the setting up of practices; and to them also fell the delicate task of changing the old system by which practices were sold to one in which the retiring doctor would receive a pension instead. This brought strong opposition, for the doctor regarded his practice as a personal investment, and his realisation on it as a necessity for retirement. There was, finally, to be a Central Tribunal to deal with disciplinary matters, with final powers of dismissal, with a chairman nominated by the Lord Chancellor.

The question of reward provoked the bitterest conflict. The doctors drew their salaries from a number of sources, freely and without central control: from private practice, from panel patients, from the police and local government bodies: from insurance companies and private firms. There was a wide disparity in income which did not necessarily satisfy the medical needs of the community. Three inter-departmental committees under the chairmanship of Sir Will Spens were set up to look into the question of payment for doctors, dentists and consultants. The findings of the two latter appeared in 1948 and aroused little controversy; that for the general practitioners reported in 1946, in ample time to add fuel to the whole dispute about the relationship of the doctors to the new service. It proposed a range of income between £1,000 and £2,500, estimating that this could be achieved by a capitation fee of fifteen shillings for each patient on the doctor's list; it also recommended that in order to help young doctors and those with 'unfashionable' practices, there should be a direct payment to all doctors of £300 without regard to the number of their National Health patients.

In April 1946, when Bevan rose to move the second reading of his Bill, the doctors' fight had only just begun. The basic award recommendation of the Spens Committee aroused the fear of a salaried service; they resented the limitation on the sale of practices, and feared that political interference would result from the composition of the Executive Committees and the Central Tribunal. The Royal Assent to the Bill came in November, but the struggle went on almost up to the appointed day for the inauguration of the National Health Service on 5 July 1948, with three BMA plebiscites showing majorities, albeit declining each time, against the doctors' entry into the scheme. In April 1948 Bevan made the vital concessions, although they might more aptly be described as clarifications, for he insisted that a state medical service had never been intended and agreed to make this clear by legislation. He limited the direct salary payment to doctors setting up for the first time, promised that the chairman of the Central Tribunal should be a lawyer of very high standing, and that the Executive Committees should appoint their own chairmen as vacancies occurred.

By 5 July a majority of the doctors had applied to enter the scheme. On that date also, the Lloyd George National Health Insurance Act, like the Poor Law, was formally buried. Its successor was not fully comprehensive, although by 1952 only 1.5 per cent of the population stood outside it: the continuance of private practice and the lack of a salaried medical service did invite the two-tier service that Bevan was anxious to avoid: and the tripartite system was unwieldy and would be difficult to administer - although it is fair to say that it was the prisoner of the past, and that a properly planned service could not be implemented without a vast reorganisation of local government, like that envisaged today, involving either a return to those systems of devolution which had been briefly contemplated during the war, or the setting up of elected regional units which had once been part of Labour's policies. Once more, and even in the creation of what Harold Wilson described as 'the very temple of our social security system', there was both compromise and a difficult development from the past; yet there was far greater enthusiasm than hostility for what was the greatest single achievement in the story of the welfare state.

In associated legislation, Labour was not so successful. The separate housing ministry they had promised did not appear. Building was still tied to its prewar administration, and the rate of construction, hampered by a grave shortage of materials, was not impressive. Subsidies, however, were provided for conversions, and an imaginative use was made of prefabricated dwellings; while the interests of private tenants were protected, in a time of inflation, by the provision of rent tribunals and rent control. The Town and Country Planning Act of 1947 made planning the responsibility of the larger authorities alone, made it obligatory for them to proceed with it, and gave them much wider powers of compulsory purchase. The state, through a Central Land Board, took the power to levy a development charge on any increase in land values brought about by the prospect of lucrative development. The New Towns Act of 1946 fulfilled the promise of the Abercromby Report. In its environmental work, the Labour Government was more successful than in housing, although the degree of state control was still far from that envisaged in the radical plans put forward by Lloyd George just before the First World War.

In education, the Act of 1944 was faithfully put into force, and local authorities went ahead with the process of selection at eleven which it implied. To many supporters of the Government, this adherence to the Butler proposals would constitute, in retrospect, a missed opportunity, for they became convinced that the Act had divisive features; and that, with the independent schools in difficulties, the postwar years presented a golden opportunity to build a system of public education, free of class distinction, which would provide the basis for a new society. As in housing and in health, the broader field of education was imaginatively dealt with; an excellent Youth Employment Service was set up, and plans went ahead quickly for a vast expansion of university and technical education; but again, as in the former instances, there was a reluctance to go too far in challenging traditional and professional interests, and to interfere too much with freedom of choice. The creation of a welfare state did not, really, involve a transformation of society; it was still, to a considerable degree, a substitute for it.

THE CRISIS OF THE WELFARE STATE, 1950-55
The welfare state which emerged in 1950 was not, therefore, associated with social upheaval, and it was, predictably on that account, of mixed parentage. It would inevitably represent compromise, just as its full development had resulted, either directly or indirectly, from the interplay of the forces of growth generated by the movement for social reform itself and the pressures set up by the great historical events which had attended it, chiefly two great wars and unprecedented depression, all in the last resort dependent on political management and skill of a high order. Yet this was frequently exercised according to differing aims and assumptions. Its three characteristic statutes were prepared by men of widely divergent political beliefs: the Education Act by Butler, a Conservative: the National Insurance Act by Beveridge, a Liberal: and the National Health Service Act by Bevan, a Socialist. It was thus also an amalgam of apparently distinct measures. In social insurance, Beveridge offered the strict minimum and tied it to insurance, and benefits over this were to be given after a means test; the implied hope was that individuals would by their own efforts provide more for themselves. Bevan wanted to provide the optimum, the best available, and it was to be offered unconditionally; there should have been no need to provide anything more, for his chief aim was to free all citizens from all anxiety about the cost of ill-health. The Socialism of the one clearly went further than the Liberalism of the other. The gap is narrowed, however, if it is remembered that Beveridge assumed that there would be a free and universal health service; and while, with his concern for an insurance basis and a subsistence minimum, he belonged to the past, in respect of universal coverage and comprehensive protection within a single scheme, he was looking to a future in which many European countries have copied him. There was, between the two, the common ground that social help should be rendered by society as a whole. This became, in fact, the assumption of the nation, but the differences in spirit which remained between the two main components of the welfare state, between the Beveridge and Bevan concepts, and the shortcomings which became evident in each, would give plenty of scope after 1950 for there to be considerable debate about just how society should fulfil its obligations.

For political and moral issues were not dead, and the period after

1950 saw the beginning of a critical reappraisal. Although a new society had emerged, there were many who saw it as the end of an evolutionary process. To some extreme Conservatives and Liberals, the Labour legislation had been simply an *ad hoc* response to a period of short-term difficulty, and they believed that it would not be needed with the return of affluence under normal economic conditions, the crutches discarded when the British people had learned once more how to walk on their own feet **(56, 69)**. Others saw it merely as a beginning, as the centre-piece of a new social order, particularly those who had led in its creation during and after the war **(68)**. Once more, the middle way would be found. The welfare state of the late 1940s was not a once-for-all creation, and neither could its fundamental assumptions be thrown away. While it clearly contained much that belonged to the past, it had, since equilibrium in matters of social reform can never be reached, to provide also some kind of stepping-stone into the future.

The prospects, in 1951, for a general reconstruction of society, were by no means propitious. Many of the extreme supporters of Labour were already frustrated by opportunities missed, and by the provision, especially in health and education, of what Arthur Marwick happily called 'escape routes from Utopia' **(6)**. Further retreat seemed likely with the Korean War, which began in 1951 when economic recovery seemed to be at hand, a war big enough to harm the economy without providing the stimulus to transform society. Resources were diverted to war; the import bill rose, and a serious balance of payments deficit developed which led to a sterling crisis in July. There was an apparent need to cut back public expenditure, and the result was the imposition of personal charges on spectacles and dentures which would yield £13 million. There was a division in the Labour leadership, already weakened by the deaths of Cripps and Bevin, and by the illness of Attlee. Aneurin Bevan, Harold Wilson and John Freeman resigned in protest, and in his resignation speech the former Minister of Health underlined the issues involved. He believed that the requirements of defence should make no inroads upon the social services or the standard of life of the British people — for the two were becoming clearly inseparable — and that the involvement in Korea would damage the economy which had to sustain them. The question of competing claims on the economy, and the fundamental strength of the economy itself, would be vital to the extension — or contraction — of the welfare services. Beneath these arguments also are the doubts, expressed by Sydney Silverman in the course of the National Insurance Debate of 1946, about whether true social security could be obtained without fuller economic control of the whole resources of the nation [**doc. 27**].

Yet the time for this comprehensive approach seemed to have gone; the only prospect for the future was in compromise. Even before Korea, the Labour initiative had been exhausted, and a number of its leaders were aware of a growing concern about too great a degree of state intervention, and a wide irritation with government control. They had themselves taken the lead in a dismantling process which had begun in 1948, and although the Conservatives removed the fear that they might undermine the system of welfare completely, when they returned to power under Churchill in 1951 the process of reappraisal would be accelerated. They would, clearly, be more sympathetic to demands for more freedom both in the economy and in the social services, provided that society still met its basic needs, and they would, in the Peelite tradition, be more inclined to rely upon material improvement as the surest way to raise the general standards of the people. To the demands of limited war and continued inflation, and to the exigencies of recurring economic crises, there must now be added the limitations of personal freedom and affluence upon the development of a welfare society.

A long period of Conservative rule opened in 1951, and there can be little doubt that for much of this time their policies reflected the feeling of the people. It is not enough here to point to a growing impatience with controls. That Labour did not inaugurate a change in the social structure of the nation was, paradoxically, partly due to its success in changing the outlook of the working people and in bringing considerable mobility between the classes. The process of the middle of the nineteenth century was to some extent repeated as the group which may be defined as 'middle-class' was growing visibly, and, with greater educational and vocational opportunities, recruiting from below; it was extending, therefore, the middle-class traditions of social and economic independence. The working class itself had won a vital economic right with the assumption of full employment, and Labour had given it an almost complete social security. It would thus cease to be a powerful driving force in the pursuit of further social and economic change while the conditions of the 1950s were maintained.

For all these reasons the future development of the social services would be associated not with social upheaval but with what has been termed 'social engineering'. The politicians would not be silent, but would often be uninformed, or guided by prejudice or intuition; and with the rapid growth of the new and complex discipline of sociology, the views of the social scientist would become equally important. In this sense, the social security system first suggested by Beveridge bore the limitations of its origins. It had been developed as part of the war on poverty and was designed to provide mere subsistence for a large number of people. By the mid 1950s, however, society had undergone great social and economic changes, and the general acceptance of the doctrine of full employment had changed the emphasis in social discussion from unemployment benefits to retirement pensions. In this sense, was the minimum enough?

In the National Health Service another weakness was even earlier apparent. While the social insurance scheme was well in solvency in the early 1950s, there was some concern about the cost of the Health Service. In 1952 further personal charges were introduced to meet increases in the cost of drugs and administration, and to cover the generous Danckwerts award to the general practitioners. An anxious Conservative Government set up the Guillebaud Committee in 1953 to examine the matter; it saw no grounds for charges of extravagance, and could suggest few ways of cutting costs that would not harm the efficiency of the service **(16)**. Rising costs, it concluded, were due to a general inflation, and further awards by the Pilkington Commission of 1960 and the Kindersley Review Body in 1963 would underline the assumption of Aneurin Bevan that a good service would have to be paid for.

In the debate of the mid 1950s, Enoch Powell and Iain Macleod made a cogently argued attack on the assumptions of the welfare state, and the universality of the social services **(67)**. The burden of the charge was that they were overreaching themselves; insurance benefits had dropped below subsistence level, and thus there was a wide recourse to National Assistance. The butter was being too thinly spread; scarce resources should be used with greater care, and given, after a stringent test, to those who really needed them. *The Times,* in February 1952, called for a re-examination of the whole basis of the social services, and Professor Titmuss, in a broadcast comment on the views of Powell and Macleod, echoed the feelings of those who saw the welfare state in danger and who feared a reversion to the pre-Beveridge era **(68).** The controversies of these years provide a perfect illustration of the welfare state at the crossroads.

PART THREE

Assessment

Assessment

The reaffirmation of Conservative power in 1955 threw a significant question mark over the future of the welfare state. The electorate, it appeared, was in a mood to doubt the wisdom of retaining unmodified a costly barrier against a basic poverty which seemed to be receding, and much was heard about moving some of the cost of social provision back on to private shoulders, of charging for it according to means, even of releasing those who wished from the system of compulsory insurance. The belief that both national and individual enterprise were being sapped by a heavy burden of taxation, and the attack on universality, marked a retreat from the idealistic view of the welfare state which regarded freedom from want as a prime social objective. The new mood was reflected in such statements as: 'We must ensure that the existing social services have built into them the mechanism that is necessary to enable them to contract' **(69).**

The debate was, in essence, between those who saw the welfare state as politically undesirable, and those who looked beyond necessity and believed that it contained political and philosophical, as well as social, values. On neither side were the arguments susceptible to exact proof. While the question of cost was vital, it was impossible to pretend that the social services were not paid for, in some way, by individuals, nor could it be proved that universal provision made the nation less self-reliant, or that while public spending was harmful, private spending was not. The resources of the state were, after all, supporting both public and private enterprise, and were assigned alike, for example, to the relief of poverty and to the indirect increase in personal wealth which came from tax relief on interest charges, pension funds, and so on. The Royal Commission on Taxation of 1954 had thrown considerable doubt on the view that high taxation lessened incentive; and it seems impossible, as far as the Health Service was concerned, that wider personal choice and the opportunity of withdrawal would have been consistent with the preservation of the basic framework necessary for good health for all. Their introduction would almost certainly have brought back an unacceptable level of discrimination; the evidence of the voluntary schemes operating in North America was not encouraging, nor could it really be envisaged that the unfortunates of society could ever do without their 'crutches'. At bottom, the debate rested on political belief, even prejudice; and the most important contribution it has made to discussion about the future of the social services has been in the reinforcement of the case for a scrupulous selectivity in their application, involving the seeking out of real need and dealing with it effectively. In this respect, the much more informed social investigations of the 1960s have thrown much more light upon this matter than the naïve, uninformed, and largely political arguments of the 1950s; and the burden of their findings is that a broadly universal provision of welfare is the only possible basis for a more intelligent selectivity **(60)**.

For the debate on the necessity for a welfare state was soon to become irrelevant. The early 1960s gave pause to the belief that affluence by itself could remove social distress, and a more sophisticated approach to the matter produced clear evidence that basic poverty had not been buried, that it could exist side by side with the welfare policies and affluence which had marked the growth of British society since the war, and, what was worse, could even be a consequence of them **(63)**. At the same time, as Britain began the long approach to Europe, it became aware that its social provision did not compare at all well with those of the members of the E.E.C., where the trend was towards, rather than away from, the statutory services. The I.L.O. estimate of 1961 was that the proportion of Britain's national income devoted to welfare was less than that of any of the Six, and there was little evidence, either, that this greater expenditure had put any real brake on economic development. A mood of national introspection and reappraisal developed in the early 1960s. Society, it was widely felt, was out-of-date: there were great differentials in wealth and status: standards of public conduct and responsibility seemed to have slipped. For various reasons — and an impending election certainly played its part — thoughts turned to the modernisation of the nation and an expansion of the public services. In 1962 the Conservative Government announced a very considerable expenditure of £500 million over ten years on hospitals, and designated seven new universities **(17)**.

There was, moreover, a much more significant consequence of affluence than the limited political argument about individual responsibility. There was a growing awareness, as in Europe, that social support in all its forms was a charge on the total wealth of the community, as distinct from that of the Exchequer alone. Welfare, once almost entirely a political instrument, handed out by governments to ease the distress and frustrations of an individualist society was, in affluence, capable of much wider dispensation. Government did more than merely provide benefits; for, by economic intervention and a diffusion of spending, it was already altering the conditions of normal life; it salvaged dying industries and provided essential support for others, quite apart from the state-run sector over which it had direct control, and in this it was sometimes difficult to disentangle the economic from the social purpose. Industry, in a period of greater prosperity, provided social benefits which widened the purely cash relationship between employer and employee, with pensions, welfare schemes and medical care for those in work and redundancy agreements and severance pay for those forced to leave it. Indeed, the problems of long-term unemployment were sometimes met by reorganisation in which both government and industry played their part. This social partnership seemed much stronger in the countries of the European Community, where it was often embedded in some variation of the 'payroll tax', and it may well figure more prominently in the formulation of social policy in Britain. Affluence, finally, raised the status and expectations of the working people; they were now in fuller social and economic membership of society, and as their everyday demands grew more sophisticated, so did they look for more than a basic provision for their social needs. This whole process brought new standards of wellbeing which depended not only upon state welfare, but upon the wealth and quality of the community itself. It is in this light that Professor Marshall spoke of the transition of welfare state to welfare society (28). The British welfare state, born in austerity, could survive into affluence only in this way.

How, then, in such circumstances, does society determine a man's right to a pension? It is in this light much more accurate to say that, in the words of an official of the American Social Security Organisation, 'a person's security and that of his family grow out of the work he does', rather than out of an insurance contract clearly unfulfilled or out of a somewhat metaphysical concept involving his membership of a community (28). The flat-rate principle belonged to the past of basic state welfare, and it was, perhaps ironically, the Labour Party which first put forward as early as 1957 an official plan for a more sophisticated scheme of national superannuation to replace retirement pensions at subsistence level. In 1961 the Macmillan Government introduced a more modest graduated scheme designed to add to the existing retirement benefit; contributions and benefits were not flat-rate, but scaled according to income, and contracting-out was allowed where an employer provided an occupational scheme with comparable benefits. Both main parties have since gone on to develop this theme, although they have differed in the means of securing the graduated retirement pension and in their attitudes to subsistence benefits. There is a general left-wing

Assessment

suspicion of any scheme which will carry into retirement the inequalities
of workaday life; although it is equally valid to point out that the
existence of a bare state scheme alone was by itself divisive when set
alongside private schemes that offered more. A wider scheme, with the
state ensuring a fair return for all, would do much to limit this. In 1969
the Labour Government introduced a White Paper outlining a much
more elaborate earnings-related National Superannuation Scheme to
replace that of 1961; and in their election manifesto of 1970 occurred
the phrase which both emphasised the need for such a scheme and
pointed to the consequences of affluence and inflation: 'Flat-rate
contributions and benefits must invariably be geared to the ability of
the lowest-paid worker to enter into the insurance contract. As a result,
those on average and above-average pay would always find a steep drop
in their means upon retirement.' The Conservative Party, too, had its
plan; they won the election, and translated their proposals into the
White Paper of 1971, *Strategy for Pensions,* and the Social Security
Bill of 1972. The aim of the latter was to see that everyone had the
chance to secure two pensions – a basic one through the existing state
scheme, and either a satisfactory occupational pension or one from a
state reserve scheme, both to be earnings-related. In moving the second
reading of the Bill, Sir Keith Joseph expressed the hope that the British
trade union movement would follow the lead of their European
counterparts and take a greater interest in negotiations for occupational
pensions, and pointed out at the same time that the provision of better
schemes of this sort would place additional financial burdens on the
employers; he thus identified both sides of industry with the development of contemporary welfare.

The new stimulus of Europe may be noted in passing; but more vital
to our present theme is further evidence of the new partnership, based
no longer simply on the bald insurance contract of 1911 between state,
employer and worker, and of the process of integration in which many
of the old antitheses begin to disappear. Another essential feature of
modern social welfare is also reiterated, in that the level of benefits
created in this way depends much more directly than ever before upon
the health of the economy and upon its potential for growth. That the
responsibilities of modern governments in welfare go beyond a bare social
provision is illustrated by the failure of the Labour administrations of
1964-70, in the light of the tasks they set themselves, to make a correct
assessment of the needs and resources of the state, in spite of the brave
hopes of the National Plan, and to provide the necessary economic
growth upon which a proper expansion of the social services could rest.
Just as before 1964 the affluent society had produced great areas of

poverty, so in 1970 the proposition was still unproven that Socialism — or an approximation to it — could generate the wealth on which fully adequate social services could rest. The return of the Conservatives promised a more realistic, less doctrinaire examination of social problems. It may yet be too early to judge, but against the experience of the last twenty years it is difficult to resist the general conclusion that the progress of real welfare in the modern state depends less on the expression of social commitment, in general terms, by the major parties, than on their success, first, in finding a prices and incomes policy which is acceptable in a free and affluent society and would help to control the inflation which inhibits the growth of the total wealth of the community, and second, in rendering precise assistance to those who are shown to be in real need.

This concept of a national level of welfare diffused over several channels has extended into other fields. The National Health Service has survived with little alteration, although some may be impending with regional reorganisation. The principles of universality and optimum provision have been maintained; criticism of cost is heard less than twenty years ago, and charges have been increased less to serve political dogma than to ease the burden on the taxpayer. It has to be accepted that the medical profession will never constitute a state-salaried medical service; and that private treatment, while obnoxiously divisive to a Socialist, will exist as long as this position continues. On the other hand, its wider extension, while so many of the private schemes make it difficult for the aged or the bad risk to participate, will not be enough to provide a good service where it is most needed. A fully comprehensive service is essential to meet the special needs of the aged and the chronic sick. The private sector may well, more significantly and realistically, keep in this country many skilled practitioners and consultants, for it is argued that if the state were bold enough to impose a uniform system considerable emigration would result. Compromise between dogmas, as between public and private enterprise, seems inevitable in the political and social climate of our times.

In the environmental field this partnership also exists. Pollution, the characteristic social evil of the twentieth century, demands both government and industrial action. Housing policies, of whatever government, retain the old mixed ingredients: free private enterprise; private enterprise with public supervision; and public, largely municipal, enterprise by itself. The supply of houses depends not only on political decisions but also on the provision of credit and the availability of workers and materials in a predominantly capitalist enterprise. Government funds support both public and private sectors; the first by subsidies to local authorities, the second by tax remission.

The progress of social reform has thus advanced considerably. The social services, once thought to be residual, only for the unfortunate, now embrace the whole population; and the total wealth of the community is now mustered in support of integrated schemes which offer benefits much greater than the mere subsistence once given only by the state. Cost has become less of an issue, and there is a growing understanding that the burden on the economy is not necessarily lightened by transferring it from one side of the ledger to the other, from the public sphere to the private. Welfare policies in an affluent age have become a means by which that affluence can be better shared; and the mood of compromise is well illustrated on the political level by the fact that the two major parties have placed in charge of Social Security in recent years two very able and enlightened men in Richard Crossman and Sir Keith Joseph, the range of whose agreement, perhaps, marks a new political maturity.

The theme of compromise may be reached from another starting-point. A welfare state which has grown up in this way cannot really be charged with the destruction of the social system. There may have been some grounds for such fears in the first years of the century; but in a modern community which has remained essentially free, in which a fusion of public and private welfare has occurred, in which it is commonly asserted that the middle classes have gained greater relative benefit from the social services than the poor, where no great attempt has ever been made to limit great extremes of wealth, and in which the possession of capital is still a distinct advantage, in such a community the egalitarians may be said to have failed. Yet while the path of compromise has reached a fairly broad plateau, we should not be deceived into thinking that the movement towards integration has solved all our social problems or that there is complete agreement about the way to whatever summits remain, and the priority of future claims on the national wealth. There is still real need, much of it indeed associated with the newer tensions of a more advanced society, and there is still a vital task for properly directed social investigation to fulfil in telling us where that need is and to point to its removal. It is, perhaps, in this more mature and quieter atmosphere of today, when old political battles are dying down and the new discipline of social science has become of age, that very real steps forward can be made to meet what Professor Titmuss has described as the great challenge of our day: 'What particular infrastructure of universalist services is needed in order to provide a framework of values and opportunity bases within and around which can be developed socially acceptable selective services aiming to discriminate positively, with the minimum risk of stigma, in favour of those whose needs are greatest' **(60)**.

It is now easier to see real poverty for what it is. In terms of cash benefits the real difficulty since Beveridge has been with those who, even with their full entitlement of relief, have still earned or received less than what mere subsistence demands, and for whom earnings-related benefits mean nothing whatsoever. Beveridge's hopes for benefits at subsistence level were not realised, and when the Poor Law was abolished in 1948 the creation of the National Assistance Board perpetuated the principle of supplementary help. A new form of the divided society was appearing, for in 1966, at the same time as Mr Wilson's Government provided earnings-related benefits for un-employment, sickness, industrial injuries and widowhood, thus making it possible for the better-off to improve their lot, so did Supplementary Benefits replace National Assistance, to be converted by the Conservative Government which followed into the Family Income Supplement Scheme of 1971, with none of these doing much more than disguise the old stigmas. On the basis of the level of subsistence that Supplementary Benefits sought to reach, it is estimated that in 1966 there were five million people living in dire need **(49)**. The reasons were often ignorance and pride; and government information services have done much to educate the people; but it is still suggested that there are a million old people today who are failing or refusing to collect the supplementary benefits to which they are entitled. There are still too many workers whose incomes, even with full-time employment, fall below the F.I.S. level: those who earn so little that they gain no benefit from tax allowances, and whose National Insurance contributions represent a very high percentage of their incomes: those of the poor who are in ill-health, and those with large families: and those who fall into the 'poverty trap', where the value of a wage increase is vastly reduced, and sometimes wiped out, by the removal of their entitlement to social benefits. Others, in receipt of benefit, suffer from the 'wage-stop', the custom by which the cash relief given to an unemployed man is restricted to the amount of his net weekly earnings when at work. It clearly exists to get men to seek work; but its consequence is that when his earnings are below the full level of benefit to which he is entitled, an unemployed man will not receive it. It is not, as is sometimes suggested, in itself a cause of poverty; but as the Supplementary Benefits Commission pointed out: 'It is a harsh reflection of the fact that there are many men in work living on incomes below the Supplementary Benefit standard' **(49)**.

How, in the modern state, with a rigid and complex social security and tax system, can there be enough flexibility for this primary poverty to be relieved? A return to Beveridge, to universal subsistence, would have the effectiveness of the bludgeon, but it would not be selective and it would be very costly. Universal help is not the answer; not so much because of its wastefulness, which was the old criticism of it, but because it is now clear that while the better-off need much less than equal treatment, the very poor need much more. To reform family allowances would help only one section; while the implementation of the national minimum wage, so favoured by the trade unions, would, as Pitt saw at the end of the eighteenth century, be equally limited in its effect and could damage the economy as a whole. The lifting of the National Insurance contribution from the shoulders of the very poor wage earner would again add considerably to taxation. Yet the evidence is that if blanket solutions are not to be dispensed indiscriminately, then very radical changes will be necessary if this residual poverty is to be eased. It would be foolish to assume that it could be relieved by a great increase in the rate of surtax; yet the supporters of selectivity, although they maintain that in order to counter inequality the state must be prepared to act unequally, have to show more fully how this discrimination can be best applied.

It is for this reason that some of the most radical thinking of recent years has revolved round schemes which bring taxation and social security together. As early as 1942 Lady Rhys Williams put forward a scheme, since developed, to produce what is termed a 'social dividend' in this way; and of more immediate importance are plans for income redistribution which are generally placed under the heading of Negative Income Tax. The principle is by no means new, for it existed in Speenhamland, and again it makes the attempt to fuse sensibly the social security and taxation systems. For the perennial problem of modern governments is that they collect taxes of all kinds, assessed on the basis of all sorts of allowances, with the one hand, and return them in the other in the form of a large variety of means-tested benefits, often, of course, to the same people, and at the cost of maintaining a large and expensive administrative machine which is not without its pitfalls for the very poor. The essence of negative income tax is the fixing of a 'break-even' rate, at which no taxes are paid and no allowances are drawn, to be assessed in the same way as the present income tax coding number. Those whose incomes fell below this line would pay no tax, and would receive a cash allowance to bring them up to it; those whose incomes exceeded it would be taxed progressively in the normal way. It could, properly administered, make a vital contribution to positive welfare, easing the anomalies of supplementary benefits and doing much to help those with large families; and the government of the day could, at a stroke and by a change in tax levels, tender direct help to those in need; but whether it would be so effective in the assistance of those out of work is doubted. The idea of swift and automatic social improvement is attractive, but Professor Titmuss believed, on the other hand, that this sort of selectivity, based on gross money incomes arrived at, perhaps belatedly, after the sort of value judgments which the assessment of allowances requires, is not enough to deal with immediate, individual deprivation: 'The computer code number proposal is not, and never can be, the answer to child poverty' **(60)**. Inevitably, again, there will be compromise.

In October 1972 came the outlines of such a compromise with the Conservative Government's Green Paper on a tax-credit scheme which would involve a wide reform of social security and taxation, and which the Chancellor of the Exchequer described as the biggest single step forward in these fields since Beveridge in 1942 and the introduction of PAYE in 1943 **(21)**. It will be examined by a Select Committee, which may well increase the chances of all-party agreement on these lines. It would abolish PAYE coding, together with a wide range of allowances – from tax allowances, through family allowances, to Family Income Supplement. On the basis of personal and family circumstances, everyone would be assigned a credit which would replace income tax allowance. Almost all income would be taxable, including pensions, sickness and unemployment pay – although not F.I.S. – at a single rate of 30 per cent. If the amount of tax payable exceeded the credit given, this would be deducted by the employer, as now; if the credit exceeded the tax, as it would do in the case of the poor, the difference would be added to income.

The contribution of this plan to welfare, as with Negative Income Tax, is that it gives the benefit of tax allowances to all, particularly to those for whom, under the present scheme, they are irrelevant. It would also minimise the disastrous effect of a normal pay increase on the condition of the lower-paid worker in removing many of his means-tested benefits, although it would not affect what would happen, in the same circumstances, to his claims to rent and rate rebates and to free school meals. It would not in any respect be fully comprehensive, because it would not affect those below a low level of income – tentatively suggested in the Green Paper as £8, or a quarter of the average industrial wage; here special benefit provisions would have to continue, for the sponsors of the plan saw little point in splitting the task of welfare between tax credits and social security. It is here that the scheme will fail to reach selectively to the very depth of poverty, and it is in this respect that it has been most severely attacked by the supporters of universality. Yet it does offer hope for the very poor. On the basis of the figures given in illustration by the Green Paper, it would add £1,300 million to the present tax bill; a good deal of this would be received by those now in dire poverty, and some would go in bringing the first child in the family into benefit; while the remainder would be put to improving the lot of every citizen, so that it would become generally acceptable to the community as a whole. It would in this way, if taken alongside an acceptable earnings-related pensions scheme, increase the forces of integration and compromise which have been a marked feature of the recent development of the social services.

It has even more to recommend it, for it illustrates the other essential feature of that development. The scheme has a high degree of relevance to the wider health of the economy; to the vital question of inflation; and to the quest for acceptable economic controls without which all social benefits are at risk. The Green Paper appeared during the long and inconclusive negotiations between Government and trade unions which attempted to secure such a policy, and it marks a contribution to the elimination of the poverty trap which leads powerful unions to press for large pay increases that will offset loss of benefits, but which could also distort the economy. The programme in the Green Paper may not avert this, for it does not reach to the limits of basic poverty; but it does much to reaffirm the essential links between taxation, social security and the economy at large, and may, at the very least, provide a springboard to further achievement.

Such progress may well bury some of the more obvious aspects of the debate over selectivity and universality. Cash, provided the resources and machinery of modern society are going to be adequate, has become distinctly less important — and certainly less topical — than the question of care, and it is sometimes in the most affluent societies that social conditions are at their worst. For while, in the 1972 edition of *Social Trends,* the annual survey produced by the Government Statistical Service, there is ample evidence of an increasing personal and national affluence over the last decade, there are marked signs of a decline in what may be termed non-material satisfactions (20). The record shows, dismally, more divorces, more illegitimate births, more abortions, and more crimes of violence; and from other sources comes evidence of wider infirmity from drugs and drunkenness. There is a strong impression that beyond the economic sphere there is a new fragmentation in society, in which personal incapacity and loneliness are among the greatest social problems of our times. We are faced now with the social consequences of affluence rather than with those of poverty.

Care is a word of wide meaning. It is warmer than welfare, in the provision of which, within the limits of an out-of-date system, the state has become reasonably efficient. For the individual, it means a better-informed understanding of his problems, and of the full consequences of the inequalities in the distribution of wealth; a much more sympathetic treatment of the infirm, whether physically or mentally afflicted, or the victims of the social pressures of our times; and guidance towards the better and fairer use of the social services available to him. In a wider context, it must involve the thorough reorganisation of the environment in which so many of these social casualties are made: of the depressed and dying areas of cities, where schools, hospitals and welfare services are often at their worst, and where the pressure of the relatively new problem of immigration is at its greatest. This new concern has many manifestations, particularly in the development of the voluntary services in partnership with the statutory ones; in the growth of community care; and in the movement towards a reintegration of the social services whose fragmentation was in part a consequence of the break-up of the old Poor Law. The growing prestige of the welfare services, both voluntary and statutory, is making real progress possible; and even as long as ten years ago the 44th Annual Report of the National Council for Social Service suggested that the welfare society had emerged as the logical successor to the welfare state, where legislative action on the part of government would be reinforced by the extension of community care. When the last Labour Government asked Seebohm to report on the best method of setting up a family welfare service, the result was a broad recommendation that it should continue on these lines [doc. 28].

Seebohm insisted that the problem of the individual was often the problem of the family, and recommended the amalgamation at local level of many of the existing separate welfare agencies into unified social services departments, and the emergence of one social worker who was equipped to deal with the several needs of any one family group. The new departments should be given the power to spend – a reintegration of cash payments and welfare services that was a feature of the old Poor Law. The acceptance of this broad principle will make it easier for the Department of Social Security, if relieved of much of the burden of national welfare payments by the adoption of some form of tax-credit scheme, to supervise properly directed local spending; for the functions of the new departments would be not only to relieve and prevent personal distress and disability, but to create a better physical and social environment in which people would find it more agreeable to live and work. There would be full encouragement of local participation, the

81

necessity for greater skill and satisfaction in local government, and a more precise estimate of local need than the remote central authority could provide. There would, in short, arrive a greater personal involvement in the affairs of the immediate neighbourhood which would accord with the demand for 'community politics' which is so often heard today. The wheel would turn full circle back to the better manifestations of the Poor Law in so far as it insisted on local care and responsibility.

Social Services Departments of this sort were established in 1971, and their preventive task seemed to be stressed by Sir Keith Joseph when he attacked what he called the 'cycle of depression' by which the neglected children of today become the neglectful parents of tomorrow. So far, the directors of these departments are prone to claim that specific grants have not been forthcoming, in spite of a projected increase in social service spending of 10 per cent each year; that they are being asked to do tomorrow's work with yesterday's equipment; that there is a shortage of trained social workers because of the reluctance of some local government bodies to take up new ideas; and that they are still too much concerned in the rescue of casualties and not enough in prevention and community care. For all this, however, they provide a real hope for the personal community welfare service of the future. The ideals they and the Seebohm Report express may well, in their call for a new community sense, with its members involved in the wellbeing of others, open the way to an even fairer society which, with material needs largely met, can show the way to deeper personal happiness and satisfaction.

PART FOUR

Documents

The Elizabethan welfare state

Professor Tawney here defines one of the essential characteristics of the Elizabethan Poor Law. It was associated with other forms of state action, and part of a comprehensive social policy to which the twentieth century has returned.

In England, after three generations in which the attempt was made to stamp out vagrancy by police measures of hideous brutality, the momentous admission was made that its cause was economic distress, not merely personal idleness, and that the whip had no terrors for the man who must either tramp or starve. The result was the celebrated Acts imposing a compulsory poor-rate and requiring the able-bodied man to be set on work. The Privy Council, alert to prevent disorder, drove lethargic justices hard, and down to the Civil War the system was administered with fair regularity. But the Elizabethan Poor Law was never designed to be what, with disastrous results, it became in the eighteenth and early nineteenth centuries, the sole measure for coping with economic distress. While it provided relief, it was but the last link in a chain of measures - the prevention of evictions, the control of food supplies and prices, the attempt to stabilize employment and to check unnecessary dismissals of workmen - intended to mitigate the forces which made relief necessary. Apart from the Poor Law, the first forty years of the seventeenth century were prolific in the private charity which founded alms-houses and hospitals, and established funds to provide employment or to aid struggling tradesmen. The appeal was still to religion, which owed to poverty a kind of reverence.

Religion and the Rise of Capitalism, Penguin, 1938, p.260.

The Speenhamland decision

Minutes of the Berkshire Justices, meeting at Speenhamland, Newbury, on 6 May 1795.
6th May 1795. BERKSHIRE, to wit.

At a General Meeting of the Justices of this County, together with several discreet persons assembled by public advertisement, on Wednesday the 6th day of May 1795, at the Pelican Inn in Speenhamland (in pursuance of an order of the last Court of General Quarter Sessions) for the purpose of rating Husbandry Wages, by the day or week, if then approved of, Charles Dundas, Esq., in the Chair,[1]

RESOLVED UNANIMOUSLY,

That the present state of the Poor does require further assistance than has been generally given them.

RESOLVED,

That it is inexpedient for the Magistrates to grant that assistance by regulating the Wages of Day Labourers, according to the directions of the Statutes of the 5th Eliz. and 1st of James: But the Magistrates very earnestly recommend to the Farmers and others throughout the county, to increase the pay of their Labourers in proportion to the present Price of Provisions; and agreeable thereto, the Magistrates now present have unanimously resolved, that they will, in their several divisions, make the following calculations and allowances for the relief of all poor and industrious Men and their families, who to the satisfaction of the Justices of their Parish, shall endeavour (as far as they can) for their own support and maintenance.

That is to say,

When the Gallon Loaf of Second Flour, weighing 8lb. 11ozs. shall cost 1s.

Then every poor and industrious Man shall have for his own support 3s. weekly, either produced by his own or his family's labour, or an allowance from the poor rates, and for the support of his Wife and every other of his family, 1s. 6d.

When the Gallon Loaf shall cost 1s. 4d.

Then every poor and Industrious Man shall have 4s.

---

[1] The names of nineteen others, of whom seven were clergymen, follow.

weekly for his own, and 1s. 10d. for the support of every other of his family.

And so in proportion, as the price of bread rises or falls (that is to say) 3d. to the Man, and 1d. to every other of the family, on every 1d. which the loaf rises above 1s.

'Berkshire Sessions Order Book' (1791-95), pp. 434-6 in *English Historical Documents,* Eyre & Spottiswoode, xii, (ed. G.M. Young W.D. Handcock) 1956

document 3

The condition of the Early Victorian poor

This extract from the famous Report of 1842 illustrates that vital factor in nineteenth century social reform - the achievement of 'safe and necessary' measures to preserve the fabric of existing society.

Whenever the adult population of a physically depressed district, such as Manchester, is brought out on any public occasion, the preponderance of youth in the crowd and the small proportion of aged, or even of the middle aged, amongst them is apt to strike those who have seen assemblages of the working population of other districts more favourably situated.

In the course of some inquiries under the Constabulary Force Commission as to the proportions of a paid force that would apparently be requisite for the protection of the peace in the manufacturing districts, reference was made to the meetings held by torchlight in the neighbourhood of Manchester. It was reported to us, on close observation by peace-officers, that the bulk of the assemblages consisted of mere boys, and that there were scarcely any men of mature age and experience, who, it was stated, generally disapproved of the proceedings of the meetings as injurious to the working classes themselves. These older men, we were assured by their employers, were intelligent, and perceived that capital, and large capital was not the means of their depression, but of their steady and abundant support.

... On inquiring of the owner of some extensive manufacturing property, on which between 1000 and 2000 persons were maintained at wages yielding 40s. per week per family, whether he could rely on the aid of the men of mature age for the protection of the capital which furnished them the means of subsistence? he stated he could rely on them confidently. But on ascertaining the numbers qualified for service as special constables, the gloomy fact became apparent, that the proportion of men of strength and of mature age for such service were but as a small group against a large crowd, and that for any social influence they were equally weak. The disappearance by premature deaths of the heads of families and the older workmen at such ages as those recorded in the returns of dependent widowhood and orphanage, must to some extent practically involve the necessity of supplying the lapse of staid influence amidst a young population by one description or other of precautionary force.

In the metropolis the experience is similar. The mobs against which the police have to guard come from the most depressed districts; and the constant report of the super-intendents is, that scarcely any old men are to be seen amongst them. In general they appear to consist of persons between 16 and 25 years of age. The mobs from such districts as Bethnal Green are proportionately conspicuous for a deficiency of bodily strength, without, however, being from that cause proportionately the less dangerously mischievous. I was informed by peace officers that the great havoc at Bristol was committed by mere boys.

The facts indicated will suffice to show the importance of the moral and political considerations, viz., that the noxious physical agencies depress the health and bodily condition of the population, and act as obstacles to education and to moral culture; that in abridging the duration of the adult life of the working classes they check the growth of productive skill, and abridge the amount of social experience and steady moral habits in the community: that they substitute for a population that accumulates and preserves instruction and is steadily progressive, a population that is young, inexperienced, ignorant, credulous, irritable, passionate, and dangerous, having a perpetual tendency to moral as well as physical deterioration.

The Report on the Sanitary Condition of the Labouring Classes (1842), in *ibid.*

The Factory Inspectorate

Leonard Horner was a member of the Factory Commission of 1833 and subsequently became one of the four original inspectors. By 1836 he was in charge of the vital area of the north and Midlands, supervising some 2,700 factories and the welfare of some 250,000 workers. The inspectors played a highly important role in the formulation of policy - in this case, over the clarification and enforcement of the Factory Act of 1844. This was not his only complaint, and in the end he helped to secure a modification of the law.

[a] *10th August 1848, Horner to Cornewall Lewis, at the Home Office*
I have had the honour to receive your letter of the 5th Inst. intimating to me that Sir G. Grey thinks it inexpedient that I should lay informations against Millowners for a breach of the letter of the Act as to the employment of Young Persons by relays in cases where there is no reason to believe that such young persons have been actually employed for a longer time than that sanctioned by law.

I beg you will assure Sir George Grey that I have every disposition to follow any instructions he may think it advisable to give me as far as I am able; but believing that he is not fully aware of the consequences that must result from my allowing the employment of young persons by relays in a manner contrary to the 26th and 52nd Sections of the Act of 1844 I feel it my duty to make the following statement.

My firm conviction is that under any modification which I have ever seen or can imagine, the employment of young persons by relays must render nugatory the main purpose of the law which imposes restriction upon their hours of work, and that acting contrary to the above named Sections is not a mere disobedience of the 'letter of the Act', but a violation of its spirit and scope, and of enactments which form necessary and indispensable adjuncts of the main restrictive enactment. All my experience up to the present hour, has satisfied me that a licence to work young persons by relays and a law restricting their labour to a given number of hours, evasions of which can practically be prevented, are two things which cannot co-exist. I cannot illustrate what I have now stated better than by the case of Messrs. Jas. Kennedy & Co. which was heard last week by the Manchester Bench of Magistrates. So far as I know, the young persons in their Mill do not, technically, work more than 10 hours a day, but practically they are engaged in their occupation nearly 13½ hours exclusive of their mealtimes.

[b] 9th January 1849, Cornewall Lewis to Horner.
Sir George Grey sees no way of settling the question but by an Act of Parliament, and it is his intention to bring in a Bill for that purpose at the commencement of the Session. *Minutes of the Statutory and Special Meetings of the Factory Inspectors*, ii, 384-7, 412.

document 5

The Education Act of 1870

Speech by W.E. Forster, Vice-President of the Council, introducing the Act in the House of Commons, 17 February 1870

The beginning of a national system of education marks a vital stage in the advance of collectivism in the second half of the nineteenth century.

More or less imperfectly about 1,500,000 children are educated in the schools that we help - that is, they are simply on the registers. But, as I had the honour of stating last year, only two-fifths of the children of the working classes between the ages of six and ten years are on the registers of the Government schools, and only one third of those between the ages of ten and twelve. Consequently, of those between six and ten, we have helped about 700,000 more or less, but we have left unhelped, 1,000,000; while of those between ten and twelve, we have helped 250,000, and left unhelped at least 500,000. Some hon. members will think, I daresay, that I leave out of consideration the unaided schools. I do not, however, leave them out of consideration; but it so happens – and we cannot blame them for it – that the schools which do not receive Government assistance are, generally speaking, the worst schools, and those least fitted to give a good education to the children of the working classes. . . .

Now, what are the results? They are what we might have expected; much imperfect education and much absolute ignorance; good schools become bad schools for children who attend them for only two or three days in the week, or for only a few weeks in the year; and though we have done well in assisting the benevolent gentlemen who have established schools, yet the result of the State leaving the initiative to volunteers, is, that where State help has been most wanted, State help has been least given, and that where it was desirable that State power should be most felt it was not felt at all. In helping those only who help themselves, or who can get others to help them, we have left unhelped those who most need help. Therefore, notwithstanding the large sums of money we have voted, we find a vast number of children badly taught, or utterly untaught, because there are too few schools and too many bad schools, and because there are large numbers of parents in this country who cannot, or will not, send their children to school. Hence comes a demand from all parts of the country for a complete system of national education, and I think it would be as well for us at once to consider the extent of that demand.

Quoted from *A History of Education in Documents, 1860-1963,* by J.S. McClure, Chapman & Hall, 1965.

document 6

The campaign for the Unauthorised Programme

The impatience of Joseph Chamberlain with the 'laissez-faire' tradition of the Liberal Party, together with his awareness of the power of the new electorate, again foreshadows the development of collectivist policies.

What is the object of this political struggle to which so many of us are giving our time, our labour, our money, and sometimes our health and our lives? If you are to believe some persons, it is a very poor and paltry business; it is a mere contest between the kites and the crows, a poor contention for place and power, animated by the basest and most unworthy motives. I suppose that those who are ready to attribute this meanness to their opponents must feel that under other circumstances they could be guilty of it themselves. But I am glad to believe that the majority of public men in Great Britain are animated by nobler and more worthy objects.

Politics is the science of human happiness, and the business of a statesman and of politicians is to find out how they can

raise the general condition of the people; how they can
increase the happiness of those who are less fortunate among
them. What are the facts of the case? I sometimes think that
we are so used to poverty and to its consequences that we
forget it or neglect it. Yet surely there is some reason to
doubt the perfection of our system when in this, the richest
country in the world, one in thirty of the population at every
moment are unable to obtain the means of subsistence without
recourse to the parish, and one in ten at the same time are on
the verge of starvation.

Joseph Chamberlain: speech in St Andrew's Hall, Glasgow, September
1885, quoted in J.L. Garvin, *Life of Joseph Chamberlain,* vol. ii,
Macmillan, 1933, p.67.

document 7

The Charity Organisation Society

*The Charity Organisation Society was set up in 1869 in order to
coordinate the work of charitable societies and the Poor Law. It was
openly 'improving' in its purpose, and it aimed at the regeneration of
the poor and of society itself. It is a typical Victorian creation; yet it
handed on to the twentieth century the basic principles of case work
and helped to bring forward the profession of the social worker. The
best statement of its aims is in the Annual Report for 1875.*

The aim of the Society is to improve the condition of the poor,
upon the following definite principles:

1. Systematic cooperation with Poor Law authorities,
   charitable agencies and individuals.
2. Careful investigation of applications for charitable aid,
   by competent officers, each case being duly considered,
   after inquiry, by a Committee of experienced volunteers,
   including representatives of the principal local charities and
   religious denominations,
3. Judicious and effectual assistance in all deserving cases,
   either through the aid of existing agencies, or, failing these,
   from the funds of the Society; those cases that cannot be
   properly dealt with by charity being left to the Guardians.
4. The promotion of habits of providence and self-reliance,
   and of those social and sanitary principles, the observance

of which is essential to the well-being of the poor and of the community at large.
5. The repression of mendicity and imposture, and the correction of the maladministration of charity.

C.O.S. Fifth Annual Report, 1875, pp. 5-6, quoted in (29), pp. 25-6.

Practicable Socialism

Canon S.A. Barnett, Vicar of St Jude's, Whitechapel, began his mission among the poor in 1873 and was a founder-member of the Charity Organisation Society. The Society always resisted the idea of state intervention in the relief of poverty; but by 1883, Barnett had come to believe that it was the only effective course, maintaining that his life in the East End had made him a Socialist.

On account of these and other causes it may be expected that poverty will be increased. The poorer quarters will become still poorer, the sight of squalor, misery, and hunger more painful, the cry of the poor more bitter. For their relief no adequate means are proposed. The last twenty years have been years of progress, but for want of care and thought the means of relief for poverty remain unchanged. The only resource twenty years ago was a Mansion House Fund, and the only resource available in this enlightened and wealthy year of our Lord is a similar gift thrown, not brought, from the West to the East.

The paradise in which a few theorists lived, listening to the talk at social science congresses, has been rudely broken. Lord Mayors, merchant princes, prime ministers, and able editors have no better means for relief of distress than that long ago discredited by failure. One of the greatest dangers possible to the State has been growing in the midst, and the leaders have slumbered and slept. The resources of civilization, which are said to be ample to suppress disorder, and to evolve new policies, have not provided means by which the chief commandment may be obeyed, and love shown to the poor neighbour.

The outlook is gloomy enough, and the cure of the evil is not to be effected by a simple prescription. The cure must be worked by slow means which will take account of the whole nature of man, which will regard the future to be as important as the present, and which will win by waiting.

Generally it is assumed that the chief change is that to be effected in the habits of the poor. All sorts of missions and schemes exist for the working of this change. Perhaps it is more to the purpose that change should be effected in the habits of the rich.

Samuel A. Barnett, 'Distress in East London', *The Nineteenth Century,* November 1886, reprinted in Michael Goodwin, *Nineteenth Century Opinion,* Penguin, 1951, pp. 66-7.

document 9

Shaw on poverty

Shaw here makes his famous attack on poverty and on the shortcomings of the religious charity which sought to relieve it. Beneath the dramatic cynicism are the hints of the truths which helped to stir the twentieth-century conscience and to goad the state into action, and also of the effects of affluence upon the working people.

UNDERSHAFT: I fed you and clothed you and housed you. I took care that you should have enough money to live handsomely - more than enough; so that you could be wasteful, careless, generous. That saved your soul from the seven deadly sins.

BARBARA *(bewildered):* The seven deadly sins!

UNDERSHAFT: Yes, the deadly seven. *(Counting on his fingers)* Food, clothing, firing, rent, taxes, respectability and children. Nothing can lift those seven millstones from Man's neck but money; and the spirit cannot soar until the millstones are lifted; I lifted them from your spirit. I enabled Barbara to become Major Barbara; and I saved her from the crime of poverty.

CUSINS: Do you call poverty a crime?

UNDERSHAFT: The worst of crimes. All the other crimes are virtues beside it: all the other dishonours are chivalry itself by comparison. Poverty blights whole cities; spreads horrible pestilences; strikes dead the very souls of all who come within sight, sound, or smell of it. What you call a crime is nothing: a murder here and a theft there, a blow now and a curse then: what do they matter? they are only the accidents and illnesses of life: there are not fifty genuine professional criminals in London. But there are millions of poor people, abject people, dirty people, ill fed, ill clothed people. They poison us morally and physically: they kill the happiness of society: they force us to do away with our own liberties and to organise unnatural cruelties for fear they should rise against us and drag us down into their abyss. Only fools fear crime: we all fear poverty. Pah! *(turning on Barbara)* you talk of your half-saved ruffian in West Ham: you accuse me of dragging his soul back to perdition. Well, bring him to me here; and I will drag his soul back again to salvation for you. Not by words and dreams; but by thirty-eight shillings a week, a sound house in a handsome street, and a permanent job. In three weeks he will have a fancy waistcoat; in three months a tall hat and a chapel sitting; before the end of the year he will shake hands with a duchess at a Primrose Leage meeting, and join the Conservative Party.

Bernard Shaw, *Major Barbara* (1905) standard edition, Constable, 1931, pp. 329-30.

document 10
Charles Booth, poverty, and 'Limited Socialism'

Booth's preliminary findings shocked him, and turned him into something more than a disinterested investigator; and statements like these gave his work far more than merely statistical interest.

[a] To the rich the very poor are a sentimental interest: to the poor they are a crushing load. The poverty of the poor is mainly the result of the competition of the very poor. The entire removal of this class out of the daily struggle for existence I believe to be the only solution of the problem of poverty. Is this solution beyond our reach?

From Booth's Second Paper to the Royal Statistical Society, *The Condition and Occupations of the People of East London and Hackney, 1887.*

[b] In taking charge of the lives of the incapable, State Socialism finds its proper work, and by doing it completely, would relieve us of a serious danger. The Individualist doctrine breaks down as things are, and is invaded on every side by Socialistic innovations, but its hardy doctrines would have a far better chance in a society purged of those who cannot stand alone. Thorough interference on the part of the State with the lives of a small fraction of the population would tend to make it possible, ultimately, to dispense with any Socialistic interference in the lives of all the rest.

From *Poverty* i, 167. Both extracts are quoted in **(45)**, pp. 96, 108-9.

document 11

The challenge of tariff reform

On 9 July 1906, the day after Joseph Chamberlain's seventieth birthday his Unionist supporters staged a great act of homage in the Bingley Hall, Birmingham. Chamberlain's speech in reply contains the essence of the renewed Conservatism he was trying to develop; a policy of national and imperial greatness, in which the condition of the poor, for too long a stain on that greatness, would be improved; and one, therefore, which represented an important challenge to the Free Trade radicalism of the revived Liberalism.

What is it that we want? What is it that we desire for our country? National prosperity. Not indeed in the sense that we covet a greater aggregation of national wealth which, for aught we know, may never be properly distributed. It is not the amount of the income tax, not the number of cheques that pass through the clearing-house that marks the progress of a nation. It is our advance towards the great Radical aspiration, 'the greatest happiness of the greatest number'. That is what we desire. That is what we, you and I, have been seeking during this past thirty years, and I have told you more than once in the course of that time that there was a greater reform than any I had yet advocated publicly before you - there was a greater reform in the future which would do more for you than all these attempts at bettering your condition, and that was a reform which would secure for the masses in the industrial population in this country constant employment at fair wages. That is an end which, with all our labour, we have not yet attained. Even now, when trade is extraordinarily active, when our opponents are boasting of record exports and imports, as though, forsooth, they were the product of any activity of theirs - I say even now there is want of employment and something much worse. There is the fact that relatively, in proportion to our competitors, in the constant struggle for existence we are getting behindhand, and when the tide of prosperity recedes, as it always has done, as it must do again, and when a time of depression follows it, we shall be the sufferers. The working classes, especially, will be the sufferers, and we shall find then that it will be impossible, without a change, to find employment for the constantly increasing population of these islands. That is the danger. I am condemned for pointing it out after we have suffered from it? Let us provide against it. Let us find the remedy.

The remedy is at hand, and if we are not too careless, too apathetic as to the future, if we are not too timid to act, I say there is even now time to hold for ourselves and our people our own trade. And we can hold it against all fair competition. And we can do more. We can extend our trade in the best markets, with our best friends. We can benefit them in trading with them, while they give us reciprocal advantage in the preference which they give for our manufactures. We can do this. We can strengthen the union. We can draw closer the growing nations, the sister states, and by a commercial union we can pave the way for that federation which I see constantly before me as a practical object of aspiration - that federation of free nations which will enable us to prolong in ages yet to come all the glorious traditions of the British race.

Quoted in (36) VI, 905-6.

document 12

Lloyd George and social reform

Lloyd George made the speech from which this passage is taken in Cardiff on 11 October 1906. It shows clearly the political considerations which helped to shape the social policies of the last Liberal Government in Britain.

But I have one word for Liberals. I can tell them what will make this I.L.P. movement a great and sweeping force in this country - a force that will sweep away Liberalism amongst other things. If at the end of an average term of office it were found that a Liberal Parliament had done nothing to cope seriously with the social condition of the people, to remove the national degradation of slums and widespread poverty and destitution in a land glittering with wealth; that they had shrunk from attacking boldly the causes of this wretchedness, notably the drink and this vicious land system; that they had not arrested the waste of our national resources in armaments, nor provided an honourable sustenance for deserving old age; that they had tamely allowed the House of Lords to extract all the virtue out of their Bills, so that the Liberal statute book remained simply a bundle of sapless legislative faggots fit only for the fire; then would a real cry arise in this land for a new party, and many of us here in this room would join in that cry. But if a Liberal Government tackle the landlords, and the brewers, and the peers, as they have faced the parsons, and try to deliver the nation from the pernicious control of this confederacy of monopolists, then the Independent Labour Party will call in vain upon the working men of Britain to desert Liberalism that is so gallantly fighting to rid the land of the wrongs that have oppressed those who labour in it.

Quoted in *English Radicalism - the Fend?*, by S. Maccoby, Allen & Unwin, 1961.

document 13

Beatrice Webb on destitution, a disease of society

Destitution, we argued, was being without one or other of the necessaries of life, in such a way that health and strength, and even vitality, is so impaired as eventually to imperil life itself. Nor is it merely a physical state. It is, indeed, a special feature of destitution in modernurban communities that it means not merely lack of food, clothing and shelter, but also a condition of mental degradation. Destitution in the desert may have been consistent with a high level of spiritual refinement. But destitution in a densely-crowded modern city means, as all experience shows, not only on-coming disease and premature death from continued privation, but also, in the great majority of cases, the degradation of the soul. Massed in mean streets, working in the sweating dens, or picking up a precarious livelihood by casual jobs, living by day and by night in overcrowded one-room tenements, through months of chronic unemployment or persistent under-employment; infants and children, boys and girls, men and women, together find themselves subjected - in an atmosphere of drinking, begging, cringing and lying - to unspeakable temptations to which it is practically inevitable that they should in different degrees succumb, and in which strength and purity of character are irretrievably lost. Anyone acquainted with the sights and sounds and smells of the quarters of great cities, in which destitution is widely prevalent - especially anyone conversant with the life histories of families below the 'poverty line' — learns to recognise a sort of moral malaria, which undermines the spiritual vitality of those subjected to its baleful influence and, whilst here and there a moral genius may survive, saddened but otherwise unscathed, gradually submerges the mass of each generation as it grows up, in coarseness and bestiality, apathy and cynical scepticism of every kind. When considerable numbers of people in such a condition are found together — still more when they are practically segregated in cities of the poor — this means that the community of which they form part is, to that extent, diseased. It is in this sense that we are entitled to say that destitution is a disease of society itself.

From *Our Partnership* (46), pp. 442-3.

document 14

The Royal Commission on the Poor Laws and the Relief of Distress, 1905-9

The extracts presented as documents 14 and 15 are from the summary of the Majority Report written by C.S. Loch for the Charity Organisation Review of February 1909. Loch was one of its principal signatories; and Sidney Webb used the summary in his contrast of the two Reports 'to escape any effect of bias against the Majority'.

What is distinctive in the Report may be summarised in a few paragraphs. The Commissioners aim at unity in the administration of relief. At present Poor Law relief is isolated from charitable relief, and new statutory relief centres have lately been created - as for instance under the Unemployed Workmen Act and the Act for the provision of meals to school children. . . . Next the Commissioners aim at the provision of large means of variation in treatment. In regard to indoor relief they propose, instead of the General Workhouse, institutional assistance of different kinds. Thus, unemployed persons - persons who require systematic work for their training and improvement, and persons for whom detention is necessary - might be properly dealt with. Accommodation for the aged, the sick and others, would in the same way be separately provided. . . Indoor or Outdoor Relief would become different methods of treatment. In great measure, the antithesis between them would disappear.

From this conclusion there follows another, a readjustment of administrative machinery. The development of Poor Law administration since 1834 has been from the parish to the Union. Set aside in the Poor Law Amendment Act as the local centre of organisation, the parish has become of less and less importance. By the Report of the present Commission a further step is taken. The Union is placed in a relation to the County or County Borough. The rate would become a County or County Borough rate. The County would be the area for institutional relief and institutional and general supervision. The Union or district would be the area for the administration of relief at the home.

. . . Again, for the purpose of voluntary relief, the Union area is taken as coterminous with the Poor Law or Public Assistance area; and the parishes, the usual areas for the administration of endowed charities, are of service once more, being drawn into relation with one another in connection with a Voluntary Aid Committee for the Union. In fact, a new Poor Law is proposed, governed by the following principles:

1. That the treatment of the poor who apply for public assistance should be adapted to the needs of the individual, and, if institutional, should be governed by classification.
2. That the public administration established for the assistance of the poor should work in co-operation with the local and private charities of the district.
3. That the system of public assistance thus established should

include processes of help which would be preventive, curative and restorative.

4. That every effort should be made to foster the instincts of independence and self-maintenance amongst those assisted.

Royal Commission - II Minority Report

The Minority Report went much further, as these extracts show - especially when it is remembered that the total destruction of the Poor Law and its replacement by specialist committees which they advocated was to be accompanied by a much wider central direction.

The dominant facts of the situation are:

(i) The overlapping, confusion and waste that result from the provision for each separate class being undertaken, in one and the same district, by two, three, and sometimes even by four separate Local Authorities, as well as by the voluntary agencies.

(ii) The demoralisation of character and the slackening of personal effort that result from the unnecessary spreading of indiscriminate, unconditional and gratuitous provision, through this unco-ordinated rivalry.

(iii) The paramount importance of subordinating mere relief to the specialised treatment of each separate class, with the object of preventing or curing its distress.

(iv) The expediency of intimately associating this specialised treatment of each class with the standing machinery for enforcing, both before and after the period of distress, the fulfilment of personal and family obligations.

We have seen that it is not practicable to oust the various specialised Local Authorities that have grown up since the Boards of Guardians were established. There remains only the alternative - to which, indeed, the conclusions of each of our chapters seem to us to point - of completing the process of breaking up the Poor Law, which has been going on for the last three decades. *(Minority Report,* p.395.)

This scheme involves that the services at present administered by the Destitution Authorities (other than those connected with vagrants or the able-bodied) - that is to say the provision for

(i) Children of school age;

(ii) The sick and the permanently incapacitated, the infants under school age, and the aged needing institutional care.

(iii) The mentally defective of all grades and all ages; and

(iv) The aged to whom pensions are awarded –

should be assumed, under the directions of the County and County Borough Councils, by

(i) The Education Committee;

(ii) The Health Committee;

(iii) The Asylums Committee; and

(iv) The Pensions Committee respectively.

That the several committees concerned should be authorised and required, under the directions of their Councils, to provide, under suitable conditions and safeguards to be embodied in Statutes and regulative Orders, for the several classes of persons committed to their charge, whatever treatment they may deem most appropriate to their condition; being either institutional treatment, in the various specialised schools, hospitals, asylums, etc., under their charge; or whenever judged preferable, domiciliary treatment, conjoined with the grant of Home Aliment where this is indispensably required.

That the law with regard to the liability to pay for relief or treatment received, or to contribute towards the maintenance of dependants and other relations, should be embodied in a definite and consistent code, on the basis, in those services for which a charge should be made, of recovering the cost from all those who are really able to pay, and of exempting those who cannot properly do so. *(Minority Report,* pp. 430-1)

Quoted from **(34)**, pp. 532-3, 540-1.

document 16

Sidney Webb on unemployment

That unemployment, even under present industrial conditions, is to a very large extent preventable was perhaps the most unexpected and certainly the most welcome piece of information which the Minority Report of the Poor Law Commission had to give to the world. Practically all previous writers, with the exception of Mr Beveridge, whose book [*Unemployment: a problem of industry,* 1909] on unemployment appeared a few weeks before the reports of the Royal Commission, accepted the phenomenon of unemployment as an inevitable accompaniment of capitalism and competitive industry, and confined their attention to the problem of how to provide for the 'out-of-work' and his family. The minority commissioners, however, after a more extensive and searching investigation than had ever before been undertaken, came to the conclusion that unemployment was mainly due to defects of industrial organisation which it is fully in the power of the state to remedy, if and when it chooses. As a consequence of this new knowledge *we are now as a nation morally responsible for the continued existence of the great army of 'out-of-works' in our midst in a far more direct and unmistakeable sense than ever before [Webb's italics].*

From an article in *The Crusade,* January 1911, quoted in **(46)**, pp. 484-5.

document 17

National Health Insurance, 1911

Lloyd George's National Health Insurance Act drew more than Conservative fire. Here Beatrice Webb sees it as little more than relief within the existing system and reiterates her belief in the much wider functions of the State.

May 26th. — George Lansbury was down here consulting with us about the amendment or postponement of Lloyd George's rotten scheme of sickness insurance. The more we examine, the less we like it, both for what it does and what it omits to do. We have written in our new book what is virtually a scathing indictment of insurance in general and the Government scheme in particular — but it will come out after the Bill is well in committee and will probably not be much attended to except by our own followers. Lansbury told us that Masterman came up to him after Lloyd George's triumphant exposition of his scheme with a pleasant jeering expression: 'We have spiked your guns, eh?' showing that he is hostile to the whole conception of the Minority Report and that the Government schemes are intended as an alternative method of dealing with the question of destitution. John Burns also goes about saying that insurance has finally 'dished the Webbs'. All of which is interesting. What remains to be seen is whether the Minority Report has come too late to stop insurance, or whether the Government scheme of insurance has come too late to stop the Minority Report! The issue is fairly joined - complete state responsibility with a view of prevention, or partial state responsibility by a new form of relieving destitution unconnected with the poor law, but leaving the poor law for those who fall out of benefit. It is a trial of strength between the two ideas. In our new book we have said our say. By the time we get back from our holiday, the matter will probably be settled one way or the other - possibly for a generation. However, if the nation finds sickness increasing and premiums going up, they may turn more quickly than we expect to prevention. And it is still possible that opposition may grow to Lloyd George's scheme and that, if he cannot get it through this session, he will have to abandon it altogether. On the whole, I should prefer the scheme abandoned rather than passed in its present form. But we do not feel inclined to agitate against it.

From (46) pp. 475-6.

document 18
Unemployment: the changing problem

Beveridge here surveys the effects of war and depression on the scheme originally conceived in 1911. The following paragraphs are extracts from his evidence to the Royal Commission on Unemployment Insurance, submitted in March 1931

The present system bears no resemblance at all either to the practice of trade unions or to the scheme of 1911 that was meant as an extension of it. Every important idea in either has gone by the board. The benefit has been made unlimited in time and practically divorced from the payment of contributions: it has become neither insurance nor a spreading of wages, but out-relief financed mainly by a tax on employment. The insurance fund has become indistinguishable from the national exchequer. All interest of employer or work-people in reducing unemployment has gone; glaringly the scheme has become in many cases a means of subsidising casual industries and insufficient wages. In the past, I, like other defenders of unemployment insurance, have often had occasion to speak of 'insurance popularly miscalled the dole'. Today, I am afraid that it might be truer to speak of 'the dole officially miscalled insurance'.

The disintegration of the insurance system is not due solely or mainly to the Act of 1930, passed by the present Government. The first step was taken when, in 1920, the system introduced in 1911 for a few selected trades was applied practically without change to all trades, no use being made of the power to exclude from the general scheme and deal by special schemes with casual occupations like dock labour or short-time industries like cotton and coal. The second and decisive step was taken when by the Act of 1927 benefit was made unlimited in duration and, for a 'transitional' period, nearly independent of any payment of contributions. The transitional provisions were extended by an Act of 1929. The Act of 1930 has simply carried to its final stage the process of merging insurance in indiscriminate relief of the able-bodied, by a further extension of transitional provisions and by abolishing the psychological requirement that the applicant should be genuinely seeking employment.

The main problem now is not that of finding an actuarial basis for the scheme as it stands. The objection to unlimited benefit given as of right is not simply or mainly that of expense, but *(a)* that money payments without conditions are an inadequate and demoralising way of dealing with prolonged unemployment, and *(b)* that the availability of such payments encourages unemployment. There would be little sense in trying to find an actuarial basis for fire insurance in a country with no fire engines and no penalties for arson.

Reprinted in *Causes and Cure of Unemployment,* (22) pp. 64-6.

document 19

Stockton-on-Tees

Evidence like that in the previous extract produced a growing commitment in academic circles to a policy of full employment to slay the Beveridge giant of idleness and to heal these new divisions in society. Equally vital to postwar developments were the experiences of the younger Conservative politicians in the same period.

I shall never forget those despairing faces, as the men tramped up and down the High Street in Stockton or gathered round the Five Lamps in Thornaby. Nor can any tribute be too great to the loyal, unflinching courage of the wives and mothers, who somehow continued, often on a bare pittance, to provide for husband and children and keep a decent home in being. Even in the South of England, the sight of wounded or unemployed ex-Servicemen begging in the street was now too common to be remarkable. Sometimes these demonstrations of misery took a more organised but none the less distressing form, such as the 'hunger marches', as they came to be called. Of these, the march of the Jarrow unemployed was the most poignant; for with the closing of Palmer's shipyard, almost the sole means of employment in the town had come to an end. There was, of course, national, local, and individual relief and assistance, on a scale unequalled in the history of this or any other country. But charity, whether of the nation as a whole or from their neighbours, was not what the men wanted. They wanted work.

Harold Macmillan, **(44)**, p.285.

document 20

The deeper significance of unemployment

The Pilgrim Trust was founded in 1931 by public-spirited men on both sides of the Atlantic. It was, during one of the worst crises in her history, an affirmation of faith in both the past and future of Britain; it was also a means of distributing grants to enterprises which would contribute to her regeneration. Inevitably, considerable help was given to the voluntary societies which were trying to help the unemployed, and in 1933 it commissioned a full-scale enquiry into unemployment so that it could make the best possible use of its resources. The result was the authoritative 'Men Without Work', which was published in 1938 with an introduction by William Temple, then Archbishop of York.

The first three extracts illustrate the deeper problems of continuing unemployment, for, in 1936, in its 'long-term' form, it had not fallen to the level of 1929, before the depression; and the fourth makes an early case for family allowances.

The reasons, or at least some of the reasons, why long unemployment fails to go down to the 1929 level cannot be identified with conditions in certain districts or certain industries, or with differences in the extent of industrial recovery. There is a 'hard core' of long unemployment which will not be resolved by recovery alone, in every town of this country, however prosperous, however diversified its range of industries, or however much its main industry benefits from industrial trends, and wherever it is situated. The problem is of increasing social importance throughout the country and is not entirely bound up with the problem of economic activity and depression . . .

. . . Herein obviously lies one of the main dangers of prolonged unemployment. If we allow standards to be reduced, we are allowing a class to grow up that is unemployable. Poverty is not only a consequence of unemployment but a cause of it. It is this that makes the case (such as might be suggested by what we have to say about the connexion between low wages and unemployment) against a reduction of allowances unanswerable. Higher allowances alone will solve very few problems. But low allowances will certainly create them - and problems of the kind that we can least afford to create. No one denies that individual abilities count - that there are badly placed families who manage, and well placed families who do not. But there can be no reasonable doubt that prolonged unemployment does tend inevitably to lower the material standards of the families suffering from it, and that if this process goes too far that group of unemployables - unemployable not only for physical, but also for mental and moral reasons - which is the real 'hard core' of unemployment will be enlarged. . . .

. . . The depression and apathy which finally settles down in many of the homes of these long-unemployed men lies at the root of most of the problems which are connected with unemployment. It is one of the reasons why they fail to get back to work. It is one of the reasons why the majority of them 'have not the heart' for clubs or activities of other kinds, and it is one of the reasons why their homes seem so poverty-stricken. 'I don't know how it is,' said a young married woman in Blackburn, 'but these last few years since I've been out of the mills I don't seem able to take trouble, somehow; I've got no spirit for anything. But I didn't use to be like that.' One of us who saw her had little doubt 'how it was'. The woman looked thin and ill, and it was clear that what food there was was going to the children. Such a simultaneous onset of physical and psychological hardship can hardly help having serious results. . . .

. . . There seems to be no doubt whatever, therefore, that the level of wages and earnings over a considerable section of industry is low enough for there to be little financial inducement for the man with a fair-sized family to work, if he is eligible for Unemployment Assistance. Yet the conclusion reached in an earlier part of this report was that among this same section of those in receipt of assistance, their economic situation, measured by a poverty standard, deteriorates progressively with increasing size of the family, and that where there are more than one or two children there is almost always evidence of hardship. These two facts, taken together, point irresistibly to the necessity for some system of family allowances to those who are working. If earning families are living at something like the same level as that of the unemployed families we visited, they will be suffering comparable hardships, and (if the problem is regarded from another point of view) there is no possibility of getting back into employment a substantial proportion of the long unemployed until some such system is established. If it were established, it would certainly provide the additional monetary incentive needed for this particular group of men, and we have little doubt that, within a reasonable time, considerable numbers of them would return to work. On the other hand, unless something of the kind is done there is every reason to fear that the problem will grow in size rather than diminish.

From *Men Without Work* (30), pp. 13-14, 133, 148-9, 209.

document 21

War and the new society: the path to universality

It would, in any relative sense, be true to say that by the end of the Second World War the Government had, through the agency of newly established or existing services, assumed

108

and developed a measure of direct concern for the health and well-being of the population which, by contrast with the role of Government in the nineteen-thirties, was little short of remarkable. No longer did concern rest on the belief that, in respect to many social needs, it was proper to intervene only to assist the poor and those who were unable to pay for services of one kind and another. Instead, it was increasingly regarded as a proper function or even obligation of Government to ward off distress and strain among not only the poor but almost all classes of society. And, because the area of responsibility had so perceptibly widened, it was no longer thought sufficient to provide through various branches of social assistance a standard of service hitherto considered appropriate for those in receipt of poor relief - a standard inflexible in administration and attuned to a philosophy which regarded individual distress as a mark of social incapacity.

That all were engaged in war whereas only some were afflicted with poverty and disease had much to do with the less constraining, less discriminating scope and quality of the war-time social services. Damage to homes and injuries to persons were not less likely among the rich than the poor and so, after the worst of the original defects in policy had been corrected - such as the belief that only the poor would need help when their homes were smashed - the assistance provided by the Government to counter the hazards of war carried little social discrimination, and was offered to all groups in the community. The pooling of national resources and the sharing of risks were not always practicable nor always applied; but they were the guiding principles.

Acceptance of these principles moved forward the goals of welfare. New obligations were shouldered, higher standards' were set. The benefits were considerable. The community relinquished, for instance, a ten-year-old practice of not providing cheap school meals unless children were first proved to be both 'necessitous' and 'undernourished'. Better pensions were given to old people as a right and not as a concession. Certain groups - expectant and nursing mothers and young children - were singled out to receive extra allowances and special aids, not because they were rich or poor or politically vocal, but because common-sense, supported by science and pushed along by common humanity, said it was a good thing to do.

These and other developments in the scope and character of the welfare services did not happen in any planned or ordered sequence; nor were they always a matter of deliberate intent. Some were pressed forward because of the needs of the war machine for more men and more work. Some took place almost by accident. Some were the result of a recognition of needs hitherto hidden by ignorance of social conditions. Some came about because war 'exposed weaknesses ruthlessly and brutally. . . which called for revolutionary changes in the economic and social life of the country'. (Anthony Eden, M.P. (Lord Avon), in the House of Commons, 6 December 1939, *Hansard* fifth series, vol. 355, cols 756-7.)

Reports in 1939 about the condition of evacuated mothers and children aroused the conscience of the nation in the opening phase of the war; much sooner, indeed, than might have been expected from the country's experience in previous wars of changes in the conception of the nation's responsibilities towards the poor and distressed. It was in 1815 — after Waterloo — that Lord Brougham's Committee met to consider 'the Education of the Lower Orders'. It was after victory in the Boer War that inquests on the physical condition of the people were opened. It was not until the later years of the First World War that plans for reconstruction began to take shape. But the evacuation of mothers and children and the bombing of homes during 1939-40 stimulated inquiry and proposals for reform long before victory was even thought possible. This was an important experience, for it meant that for five years of war the pressures for a higher standard of welfare and a deeper comprehension of social justice steadily gained in strength. And during this period, despite all the handicaps of limited resources in men and materials, a big expansion took place in the responsibilities accepted by the State for those in need.

Richard M. Titmuss, **(33)**, pp. 506-8.

Dunkirk

Dunkirk, to many, was the symbol of the determination to put right past wrongs. 'The Times' printed the following in a famous leader only a few weeks after the evacuation.

If we speak of democracy, we do not mean a democracy which maintains the right to vote but forgets the right to work and the right to live. If we speak of freedom, we do not mean a rugged individualism which excludes social organisation and economic planning. If we speak of equality, we do not mean a political equality nullified by social and economic privilege. If we speak of economic reconstruction, we think less of maximum production (though this too will be required) than of equitable distribution.

The Times, 1 July 1940.

The Beveridge debate

The enthusiasm of the Labour Party for the Beveridge Report is reflected here in the speech made by James Griffiths in the debate of February 1943.

The plan has, among others, three great merits. First, it is comprehensive. It brings within the range of social insurance practically every citizen in this country. It brings them all in instead of dividing the country into sections and saying that one section shall be brought in and another left out. The second great merit is that it provides security from want in adversity by guaranteeing a minimum subsistence income, whatever the cause and however long the period. Lest there be here or in the country any idea that Sir William Beveridge is proposing that people shall be given such a standard of life that they will be tempted to become malingerers, I would point out that what he proposes is a subsistence income, and income upon which people can subsist, and by the instrument of insurance he provides that the subsistence income shall be related to need and based upon standards which he outlines in his Report. He ends the anomalies by which the benefit which people get in adversity depends not as now, upon the need the adversity creates, but upon how the adversity arose. The plan proposes that a minimum subsistence income shall be provided for people in adversity, whatever may be the cause and however long the period. The third great merit of the plan is that it consolidates our social insurance and allied services into a single scheme under the direction of a single Ministry and with unified administration. Therefore, it does completely fulfil the task which Sir William Beveridge was asked by my right hon. Friend to undertake.

There is the plan, and what we have to decide today is this: Are we going to accept this plan and this structure, or are we not? Believe me, it is by acceptance or rejection of the plan that we shall be judged by this nation. There will be time enough later on for crossing 't's' and dotting 'i's', but there can be no doubt that what has appealed to the people is the fact that here is a comprehensive plan to meet all contingencies and to provide this minimum income for everyone. It is because we are convinced that the nation wants this plan and that the nation ought to get it, and that we can afford it, that we have put down this Amendment.

Let me say a few words, very respectfully, upon the point that we can afford it. I suggest that the question which we ought to ask ourselves is not whether we can afford the plan, but whether we can afford to face the post-war period without it. Can we, indeed, afford to do without it? My view is that we cannot face the future, with all the colossal readjustments which it involves, without this plan. We have no right to ask our people to face those readjustments without this plan. We have made claims upon them, and since the war began we have been increasing those claims all the time. We have called our youths to the Services, and we have called our men to work. We have all joined in doing so. Let me say a personal word upon this. In the town which I am privileged to represent, thousands of men have been asked to go away from the area. I have gone there and have asked them to do so, and I have given them a pledge which I must not break. I have said to them, 'You are asked now to leave your homes and your work and your community – to leave everything for the sake of the country. It is my pledge to you that when the war is over, I will do my best to see that you are put back into decent jobs, and if decent jobs are not available, that you shall be guaranteed an income that will save you and your family from want.' We have called for sacrifices, and that is our responsibility. The response of our people has been wonderful, beyond praise, and I hope that we shall remember that we owe these people a debt that we must honour and that we shall begin to honour that debt today.

Speech in the House of Commons, 18 February 1943, *Hansard*, fifth series, vol. 386, cols 1966-67.

document 24

The unique welcome for the Beveridge Report

The Ministry of Information summarised the attitudes of the Clydeside workers in this document of 18 March 1943.

The following notes have been written specifically on the attitude of the Clydeside Workers to the Beveridge Plan, but correspondence and postal censorship reports from other areas show that similar points of view also exist in other parts of the country.

Interest in the Beveridge Plan on its publication was really tremendous. For a week or two the war news tended to take a back seat and one report says: 'There has been possibly more widespread discussion on this than on any single event since the outbreak of the war.' The publicity given to the scheme by the radio and Press together with the explanatory pamphlets on the subject, which appeared almost overnight, aroused a quite remarkable enthusiasm.

Practically everyone approved of the underlying principles, and hopes ran high that the Plan would be put into operation as soon as possible. Some workers indeed regarded the plan as an enactment. To some women for instance its reality was so actual that they were calculating how much they would be allowed to draw for their children and telling their menfolk that 'We'll draw the money and not you; you will just hand in the same pay as usual.' One woman writing to an older one at this time said, 'It's hard lines on you. I arrived at the right time.' Others who had feared wholesale disturbance after the war said, 'This will give us something to fight for and look forward to. The soldiers needn't hang on to their guns after all.'

Soldiers writing home spoke of their pleasure at the Scheme, saying, 'This gives us some heart to fight. We know that if something happens to us our wives and children will never want.'

To the critics who inquired 'Can we pay for it?' the impatient reply was given, 'We can always pay for wars, this one costs £15 million a day. We will just *have* to afford the Beveridge Plan.'

The cynics who said, 'This is just propaganda to keep us at it till the war is over' were looked upon as disturbers of the peace or as unpatriotic.

After the Parliamentary Debate the general optimism slumped badly. The slump was not immediate; in fact it was about a week after the Debate that condemnatory remarks began generally to be heard.

Confidence in the Government, in political leaders, in fact in leaders of all kinds, greatly deteriorated.

One Trade Union official recently remarked, 'I am almost ashamed to look the men in the face; they simply laugh at me when I ask them for more output.'

Nor is the workers' belief that they have been badly let-down helping to improve relations between them and their employers.

Quoted in Janet Beveridge (39), pp. 123-4.

document 25
Winston Churchill and postwar conditions

It has sometimes been said loosely that Churchill was lukewarm about the Beveridge Report. It is possible that he did not fully appreciate the nation's enthusiasm for it; yet he accepted its necessity, and in a Cabinet minute circulated on 14 February 1943 he wrote: 'This approach to social security, bringing the magic of averages nearer to the rescue of the millions, constitutes an essential part of any postwar scheme of national betterment.' It would be fairer to describe his attitude as cautious, and in the following note he had circulated to the Cabinet on 12 January 1943 there were words of warning which, in the light of the postwar burdens the social services were to have to bear, were important, and not without fulfilment.

12 JANUARY 1943

1. A dangerous optimism is growing up about the conditions it will be possible to establish here after the war. Unemployment and low wages are to be abolished, education greatly improved and prolonged; great developments in housing and health will be undertaken; agriculture is to be maintained at least at its new high level. At the same time the cost of living is not to be raised. The Beveridge plan of social insurance, or something like it, is to abolish want. The money which the wage-earning classes have saved during the war in nest-eggs or accumulated by War Savings Certificates must not lose its value.
2. Our foreign investments have almost disappeared. The United States will be a strong competitor with British shipping. We shall have great difficulties in placing our necessary exports profitably. Meanwhile, in order to help Europe, we are to subject ourselves to a prolonged period of rationing and distribute a large part of our existing stocks. We are to develop the tropical Colonies and raise the condition of their inhabitants. We must clearly keep a large Air Force and Navy, so as not to be set upon again by the Germans, and large military forces will be needed to garrison the enemy countries and make sure they do not begin again to rearm for revenge.
3. The question steals across the mind whether we are not committing our forty-five million people to tasks beyond their compass, and laying on them burdens beyond their capacity to bear. While not disheartening our people by dwelling on the dark side of things, Ministers should, in my view, be careful not to raise false hopes, as was done last time by speeches about 'homes fit for heroes', etc. The broad masses of the people face the hardships of life undaunted, but they are liable to get very angry if they feel they have been gulled or cheated. If, for instance, we raise the old age pension to £2 and other insurance benefits proportionately, and then, owing to a decline in the purchasing power of money, they find that the £2 buys no more than the 10s. formerly did, or that their nest-egg or War Savings Certificates only in fact yield a quarter of the sweat and effort which their accumulation entailed, they will feel a sense of grievance quite different from the pangs endured by mankind in its inevitable struggle for existence. It is because I do not wish to deceive the people by false hopes and airy visions of

Utopia and Eldorado that I have refrained so far from making
promises about the future.
4. We must all do our best, and we shall do it much better if
we are not hampered by a cloud of pledges and promises
which arise out of the hopeful and genial side of man's
nature and are not brought into relation with the hard facts
of life.

Winston Churchill, *The Second World War,* Cassell, 1951, iv 861-2
(Appendix F).

Clement Attlee on the National Insurance Bill, February 1946.

*In this passage, the Labour Prime Minister also relates the social services
to the needs of the nation, and examines the question of cost; the
emphasis, however, is different.*

We now recognise that, to allow, through mass unemployment,
or through sickness, great numbers of people to be ineffective
as consumers is an economic loss to the country . . . it is
interesting to see how far, in quite a short time, we have
travelled from the conception of the panic cutting-down of
the purchasing power of the masses, which was employed as
a means of dealing with the abundance crisis of 1931. . .
. . .The question is asked - Can we afford it? Supposing the
answer is 'No'? What does that mean? It really means that the
sum total of goods produced and the services rendered by the
people of this country is not sufficient to provide for all our
people at all times, in sickness, in health, in youth and in age,
the very modest standard of life that is represented by the
sums of money set out in the Second Schedule to this Bill.
I cannot believe that our national productivity is so slow,
that our willingness to work is so feeble or that we can submit
to the world that the masses of our people must be condemned
to penury. After all, this is really the payment into a pool of
contributions from employers and workers and the products
of taxation, and the payment thereout of benefits to various
categories of persons. It is a method of distributing purchasing
power, and the only validity for the claim that we cannot

afford it must rest either on there not being enough in the pool, or on the claim that some sections of society have a priority to take out so much that others must suffer want.

I am not prepared to admit either of these propositions. Where I do entirely agree is, that we can only afford it if we are prepared to utilise to the full our resources in labour and materials, our skill, our scientific inventions and our power of organisation. Therefore, this is only a part of Government policy. There is the complementary side, the reorganisation and reinvigoration of our economic life, and the increase of our overseas trade. We must secure and maintain a high level of national production. We must eliminate waste, both in production and distribution. But I entirely agree that the benefits of this Bill can only be secured if the people of this country recognise the obligation to work hard for them.

Speech in the House of Commons, *Hansard,* fifth series, vol. 418, cols 1897, 1910-11.

document 27
Sydney Silverman and the basis of the welfare state

Sydney Silverman, a true Socialist within the Labour Party, would not for this reason regard welfare as a mere palliative. He here maintains that the true foundation of a welfare state is a rigidly managed economy. This existed during the war and for some time afterwards, and it helped to create a much more tightly knit, organic community than has existed either before or since. But the conditions he postulates did not last; and when controls relaxed and when personal affluence came to be regarded as socially acceptable, a new basis for welfare had to be found. The welfare state came to be judged in terms of its market value, and many felt that its true aim should then be - as Charles Booth had suggested - the salvage merely of the casualties of society as it returned to an individualist ethic.

Silverman spoke after Attlee; his appreciation of the difficulties of welfare in a sophisticated society are somewhat more realistic.

Many speakers in this Debate have set this Bill against the background of previous social legislation and reform, and they were right to do so. I would like to set it against another background, and that is the background of the other legislation

117

for which this Government have been responsible in the last six months. The achievement of social security must be the achievement of the guarantee by the community of a minimum national subsistence level in all circumstances and against all chances and economic changes and hazards. Unless the community take full charge and full control of its resources, the mere guarantee of a weekly monetary minimum would take us no distance at all along the road to real prosperity. Had it not been for the rationing of commodities in short supply, the control of prices, the control of material resources, the control of finance, the serious and sincere endeavour to get a planned economic and industrial society into which social security had to be fitted, this subsistence monetary level would indeed have been a meaningless symbol. A guaranteed monetary minimum in a social and economic framework handed over to free enterprise, and the inevitable inflation in which that would have resulted in present conditions, would have made a mockery of the whole plan and idea. I think it would be wrong to take part in the Debate without paying tribute to that advance which this Measure represents, and without congratulating the Government upon doing it so quickly and so well.

Speech in the House of Commons, *Hansard,* fifth series, vol. 418, cols 1951-52.

document 28
The new challenge of welfare - the Seebohm Report

With the Seebohm Report of 1968, and the beginning of its implement-ation after 1970, comes a wider appreciation of the extent of social need, and the hope that social policy will reach beyond the amelioration of distress to a deeper understanding of the problems which have given rise to it.

139. We are convinced that if local authorities are to provide an effective family service they must assume wider respon-sibilities than they have at present for the prevention, treatment and relief of social problems. The evidence we have received, the visits we have undertaken, and our own experience

118

leave us in no doubt that the resources at present allocated to these tasks are quite inadequate. Much more ought to be done, for example, for the very old and the under fives, for physically and mentally handicapped people in the community, for disturbed adolescents and the neglected flotsam and jetsam of society. Moreover, the ways in which existing resources are organised and deployed are inefficient. Much more ought to be done in the fields of prevention, community involvement, the guidance of voluntary workers and in making fuller use of voluntary organisations. We believe that the best way of achieving these ends is by setting up a unified social service department which will include the present children's and welfare services together with some of the social service functions of health, education and housing departments.

140. Such a unified department will provide better services for those in need because it will ensure a more co-ordinated and comprehensive approach to the problems of individuals and families and the community in which they live. It should be more effective in detecting need and encouraging people to seek help; it should attract more resources and use them more efficiently and it will be possible to plan more systematically for the future.

141. The need for a more unified provision of personal social services has been made plain by growing knowledge and experience. There is a realisation that it is essential to look beyond the immediate symptoms of social distress to the underlying problems. These frequently prove to be complicated and the outcome of a variety of influences. In many cases people who need help cannot be treated effectively unless this is recognised. Their difficulties do not arise in a social vacuum; they are, have been, or need to be involved in a network of relationships, in social situations. The family and the community are seen as the contexts in which problems arise and in which most of them have to be resolved or contained. Similarly, residential establishments are no longer asylums, separated and insulated from the outside world. They are increasingly expected to maintain contacts with the families of those for whom they care and the communities in which they are located. To take another example, the local authority personal social services should accept the responsibility of concerning themselves with offenders and the families of offenders, co-operating for this purpose with

the probation and aftercare service, the prison welfare service, and other statutory and voluntary organisations.

142. The present structure of the personal social services ignores the nature of much social distress. Since social need is complex it can rarely be divided so that each part is satisfactorily dealt with by a separate service. In the previous chapter we rejected a number of proposals for reform because they allocated the responsibilities of departments according to age or 'types' of problems. This, we believe, reflects an artificial and rigid view of human need. An integrated social service department will impose fewer boundaries and require less arbitrary classification of problems. Of course, important administrative boundaries will remain. Responsibilities for medical care, education and housing will continue to be separate, although the problems they deal with also have an obvious social component.

From the Seebohm Report, (19), pp. 44-5.

Bibliography

GENERAL

1   Burn, W.L. *The Age of Equipoise,* Allen & Unwin, 1964.
2   Ensor, R.C.K. *England, 1870-1914,* Oxford University Press, 1936.
3   Gregg, Pauline. *A Social and Economic History of Britain from 1760 to the Present Day,* 5th ed, Harrap, 1966, and
4   Gregg, Pauline. *The Welfare State,* Harrap, 1967 (a detailed history of the social and economic development of Britain since 1945).
5   Kitson Clark, G. *The Making of Victorian England,* Methuen, 1962.
6   Marwick, A. *Britain in the Century of Total War: war, peace and social change, 1900-67.* Bodley Head, 1968.
7   Mowat, C.L. *Britain Between the Wars,* Methuen, 1955.
8   Taylor, A.J.P. *English History, 1914-45,* Oxford University Press, 1965.
9   Woodward, E.L. *The Age of Reform, 1815-70,* 2nd ed, Oxford University Press, 1962.

HISTORY OF THE SOCIAL SERVICES

Primary sources (all published by H.M.S.O.)

10 *Report of the Royal Commission on the Poor Laws, 1909* (Cd 4499).
11 *Final Report and Minority Report of the Royal Commission on Unemployment Insurance, 1932* (Cmd 4185).
12 *Social Insurance and Allied Services* (the Beveridge Report), November 1942 (Cmd 6404).
13 *Educational Reconstruction,* July 1943 (Cmd 6458).
14 *A National Health Service,* February 1944 (Cmd 6502).
15 *Social Insurance, Parts I and II,* September 1944 (Cmd 6550 and 6551).
16 *Report of the Committee of Enquiry into the Cost of the National Health Service* (the Guillebaud Report), 1956 (Cmnd 9663).
17 *A Hospital Plan for England and Wales,* 1962 (Cmnd 1604).
18 *The Development of Community Care, 1963* (Cmnd 1973).

19   *The Report of the Committee on Local Authority and Allied Personal Services* (the Seebohm Report), 1968 (Cmnd 3703).
20   *Social Trends,* 1972: later issues as they become available.
21   *Proposals for a Tax-Credit System,* 1972 (Cmnd 5116).

Secondary sources

22   Beveridge, W. *Causes and Cure of Unemployment,* Longmans, 1931.
23   Bruce, M. *The Coming of the Welfare State,* Batsford, 1961.
24   Finer, S.E. *The Life and Times of Sir Edwin Chadwick,* Methuen, 1952.
25   Gilbert, Bentley B. *The Evolution of National Insurance in Great Britain: Origins of the Welfare State,* Michael Joseph, 1966.
26   Jewkes, John and Jewkes, Sylvia. *The Genesis of the British National Health Service,* Blackwell, 1962.
27   Marsh, David C. *The Changing Social Structure of England and Wales, 1871-1961,* Routledge, 1966.
28   Marshall, T.H. *Social Policy,* Hutchinson, 1965.
29   Mowat, C.L. *The Charity Organisation Society, 1869-1913,* Methuen, 1961.
30   The Pilgrim Trust. *Men Without Work,* Cambridge University Press, 1938.
31   Roberts, D. *The Victorian Origins of the British Welfare State,* Yale University Press, 1960.
32   Rooke, P. *The Growth of the Social Services in England,* Weidenfeld & Nicolson, 1968.
33   Titmuss, R.M. *Problems of Social Policy (History of the Second World War),* H.M.S.O. and Longmans, 1950.
34   Webb, Beatrice and Webb, Sidney. *English Poor Law History, Part II:* Vols. 8 and 9 of *History of Local Government:* Part II 'The Last 100 years', first published 1929, reprinted 2nd edition 1963, Frank Cass.
35   Williams, Gertrude. *The Coming of the Welfare State,* Allen & Unwin, 1967.

BIOGRAPHY AND MEMOIRS

36   Amery, J. *The Life of Joseph Chamberlain,* vols. V and VI, Macmillan, 1969.
37   Attlee, Clement. *As It Happened,* Odhams, 1956.
38   Bevan, Aneurin. *In Place of Fear,* Heinemann, 1952 and 1961.
39   Beveridge, Janet. *Beveridge and his Plan,* Hodder & Stoughton, 1954.

40   Braithwaite, W.J. *Lloyd George's Ambulance Wagon: the memoirs of W.J. Braithwaite,* ed. H. Bunbury and R.M. Titmuss, Methuen, 1957.
41   Churchill, Randolph. *Winston S. Churchill,* vols. i and ii, Heinemann, 1967.
42   Cole, Margaret. *Beatrice and Sidney Webb,* Fabian Society (Tract 297), 1956.
43   Jones, Thomas. *Lloyd George,* Oxford University Press, 1951.
44   Macmillan, Harold. *Winds of Change, 1914-39,* Macmillan, 1966.
45   Simey, T.S. and Simey, M.B. *Charles Booth, social scientist,* Oxford University Press, 1960.
46   Webb, Beatrice. *Our Partnership,* ed. M. Cole and B. Drake Longmans, 1948.

SOCIAL POLICY AND ADMINISTRATION

47   Abel-Smith, B. *Freedom in the Welfare State,* Fabian Society,1965.
48   Abel-Smith, B. and Townsend, P. *The Poor and the Poorest,* Bell, 1965.
49   Atkinson, A.B. *Poverty in Britain and the Reform of the Social Services* (University of Cambridge Department of Applied Economics Occasional Papers), Cambridge University Press, 1969.
50   Finer, H. *The Theory and Practice of Modern Government,* Methuen 1950.
51   Goldman, P. *The Welfare State,* Michael Joseph, 1964.
52   Hall, Penelope. *The Social Services of Modern England,* Routledge, 1970.   .
53   Harvey, Audrey. *Casualties of the Welfare State,* Fabian Society, 1960.
54   Jones, Kathleen. *The Compassionate Society,* S.P.C.K., 1966.
55   Marsh, D.C. *The Future of the Welfare State,* Penguin, 1964.
56   Peacock, A.T. *The Welfare Society,* Liberal Publication Department for the Unservile State Group, 1961.
57   Robson, W.A. *The Welfare State* (L.T. Hobhouse Memorial Lecture No. 26), Oxford University Press, 1957.
58   Robson, W.A. and Crick, B. *Future of the Social Services,* Penguin, 1970.
59   Slack, Kathleen. *Social Administration and the Citizen,* Michael Joseph, 1968.
60   Titmuss, R.M. *Commitment to Welfare,* Allen & Unwin, 1968.
61   Titmuss, R.M. *Essays on the Welfare State,* Allen & Unwin, 1958.
62   Titmuss, R.M. *Income Distribution and Social Change,* Allen & Unwin, 1962.

63   Titmuss, R.M. *The Irresponsible Society*, Fabian Society, 1959.
64   Titmuss, R.M. with Abel-Smith, B. *The Cost of the National Health Service*, 1956.
65   Townsend, P. *Poverty, Socialism, and Labour in Power*, Fabian Society 1967.

PERIODICALS AND PAMPHLETS

British Journal of Sociology
The European Journal of Sociology
New Society (1962-)
Particular articles and pamphlets
On the development of the welfare state:

66   Briggs, A. 'The Welfare State in historical perspective', *European Journal of Sociology*, November 1961.

On the debate of the 1950s:
67   Macleod, Iain, and Powell, J. Enoch. *The Social Services, Needs and Means*, Conservative Political Centre, 1951 and 1954.
68   Titmuss, R.M. 'Crisis in the social services', *The Listener*, 14 February 1952.
69   Howe, Geoffrey. *The Reform of the Social Services*, Bow Group, 1960.

On the reappraisal of the 1960s:
70   Townsend, P. 'The meaning of poverty', *British Journal of Sociology*, xiii, no. 3, October 1962.
71   Lynes, T. *National Prosperity and National Assistance*, Occasional Papers in Social Administration no. 5, Codecote Press, 1962.

On contemporary issues:

72   *The Times*, 11 and 12 March 1971: the outline of a programme for a comprehensive social policy: social policy and the 'good society'.
73   *The Times*, 14 May 1971: Proposals for Welfare Reform, by Tony Lynes.
74   Titmuss, R.M. 'Social security and the Six', *New Society*, 11 November 1971.
75   Barker, David. 'Family income supplement', *New Society*, 5 August 1971.

76   *The Spectator*, 22 January 1972, 5 February 1972 and 12
      February 1972: an important series of articles on 'The Welfare
      State - thirty years on.'
77   *The Economist*, 24 May 1969: a reassessment of the Beveridge
      principles.
78   *The Political Quarterly*, January to March 1969: an issue devoted
      entirely to the questions surrounding the welfare state today.

Index